What do we think we know about learning, teaching, & especially assessment in higher education, & what this means in practice

Chris Rust

Copyright 2020 Chris Rust

Revised. All rights reserved.

ISBN: 9798682428373

DEDICATION

This book is dedicated to all those educational developers and pedagogic researchers whose work has inspired me over the years, especially those who I have worked closely with, and co-written with, but in particular David Jaques, who gave me the incredible opportunity to move to Oxford Polytechnic (now Oxford Brookes) and all that that subsequently made possible.

CONTENTS

	Acknowledgments	1
1	What do we think we know about student learning, and what are the implications for improving that learning?	3
2	Purposes and Principles of Assessment	40
3	What do we think we know about assessment: the international state of research on assessment & examinations in Higher Education	48
4	Re-thinking assessment: a programme leader's guide	73
5	Avoiding the road to hell: the need to evaluate our practice and to corroborate what we think we know	93

ACKNOWLEDGMENTS

Earlier versions of each of these chapters have been previously published separately by the Oxford Centre for Staff and Learning Development, Oxford Brookes University, UK (https://www.brookes.ac.uk/ocsld/).There is inevitably therefore some overlap and repetition between them.

Chapter 1 was first published as the Foreword in Rust, C. (Ed) (2013) *Improving student learning through research and scholarship: 20 years of ISL,* Oxford, Oxford Centre for Staff & Learning Development and subsequently as an e-book, accessed 1/9/20 at
https://shop.brookes.ac.uk/product-catalogue/oxford-centre-for-staff-learning-development/books-publications/ebooks/what-we-know-by-chris-rust-ebook

Chapter 2 was first published Rust, C. (2002) *Purposes and principles of assessment*, Learning and Teaching Briefing Papers series, Oxford Centre for Staff & Learning Development

Chapter 3 was first publlshed Rust, C. (2013) "The international state of research on assessment & examinations in Higher Education". In Bork, Reinhard (Ed) (2015) *Prüfungsforschung, Schriften zur rechtswissenschaftlichen Didaktik* 6, pp19-43, Berlin: Nomos and subsequently by the Oxford Centre for Staff & Learning Development as an e-book, accessed 1/9/20 at
https://shop.brookes.ac.uk/product-catalogue/oxford-centre-for-staff-learning-development/books-publications/ebooks/what-we-knowabout-assessment-ebook

Chapter 4 was first published Rust, C. (2017, 2020 Revised) *Re-thinking assessment – a programme leader's guide,* Oxford Centre for Staff & Learning Development, accessed 1/9/20 at
http://ocsld.brookesblogs.net/2017/12/22/re-thinking-assessment-a-programme-leaders-guide/

Chapter 5 was first published Rust, C. (2014) "Avoiding the road to hell: the importance of BeJLT and pedagogic research at Brookes (Editorial)" *Brookes eJournal of Learning and Teaching (now renamed Higher Education Journal of Learning & Teaching)*, Vol.6, Issue 1, Oxford Centre for Staff & Learning Development

1 What do we think we know about student learning, and what are the implications for improving that learning?

There is a lot of published research about student learning and this is an attempt to summarise that literature and to take stock of what we think we know already. But it comes with the following 'health warning'. It is a personal viewpoint[1] and, while I have tried to summarise ideas that I think are widely accepted across the sector, this is not to say that they would be unanimously supported.

I have grouped the theories under four headings, starting with students as learners, as student learning is after all our central focus, and then moving out to consider the ways that teaching, course design, and the wider environment can all affect the quality of the students' learning (plus an additional final 'tension' at the end). Because of space, these theories have been significantly distilled and so subtleties and different nuances within each main idea may have been lost. Similarly with the further reading suggestions, I have tended to limit them to seminal works rather than the most recent. It should also be noted that while the ideas have been separated out to make them easily accessible, many overlap and aspects merge.

---

[1] Although I am very grateful to Linda Price and John Richardson for their helpful comments and advice

Students as learners

Learning is affected by feelings (the affective domain)

What do we know?

Students have feelings, and feelings can affect learning (for good or ill) just as much as knowledge, ability, or effort. Students are far more likely to learn if they are motivated (see section below) and whether students are motivated can be significantly affected by how they feel. This relationship is neatly expounded in Maslow's hierarchy of needs, which he first proposed in 1943. The pinnacle of this hierarchy is self-actualisation (which is surely the aim of learning in higher education?) but Maslow argues that for the necessary motivation for this to take place the four more fundamental and basic needs in the hierarchy need to have been met, namely: physiological needs; safety needs; love and belonging; and esteem.

Implications for improving student learning

If the classroom is freezing cold, or hot and stuffy, or the student is lacking food or sleep it will affect their ability to learn. But the importance of Maslow's other stages may be slightly less obvious. If a student feels insecure, unknown, and effectively 'unloved'; if they are unclear about what is expected of them, if they are frightened by the assessment process, or of the possibility of being 'shown-up' and possibly humiliated in class; if they feel bored, isolated, or anxious, they are not likely to learn or perform well.

Anxious students "adopt over-cautious strategies, fall back on earlier and cruder ways of seeing the world, forget things and have trouble concentrating. Over recent years there has been a growing interest in the concept of compassion, and its potential within classrooms to increase cooperation and improve learning. Compassion is defined in neuroscience, anthropology and clinical psychology as: noticing distress/disadvantaging to others or the self AND addressing it, and is clearly linked to various capacities such as sympathy, empathy, forgiveness and warmth – as well as a core element of pro-social behaviour. Our minds have developed to be highly sensitive and quick to react to perceived threats and this fast-acting threat-response system can be a source of anxiety, depression and aggression. Studies have shown that developing kindness and compassion for self and others can help in calming down this threat system but, in addition, it actually increases feelings of contentment and well-being.[2]

The emotional tone you set through your teaching, and the attention you pay to the emotional well-being of your students, are likely to be at least as important as the teaching and learning methods you adopt and the skills you develop." [3]

Further reading

Maslow, A (1954) *Motivation and personality.* New York, NY: Harper.

Rogers, C. (1969) *Freedom to Learn: A View of What Education Might Become*, Columbus, Ohio: Charles Merill.

Rogers, C. (1983) *Freedom to Learn for the 80's,* Columbus, 2nd Rev Edition, Ohio: Charles Merill.

Vikki Hill with Dr Theo Gilbert *Compassion in Higher Education* @ The Exchange blog, available at: https://tle.myblog.arts.ac.uk/compassion-in-higher-education-vikki-hill-with-dr-theo-gilbert/

---

[2] https://tle.myblog.arts.ac.uk/compassion-in-higher-education-vikki-hill-with-dr-theo-gilbert/
[3] Gibbs, G. & Habeshaw, T. (1989) *Preparing to Teach*, Bristol: TES p38

Learning is affected by epistemological development

What do we know?

Students' learning is affected by their attitude to knowledge and what they believe knowledge to be. There are a number of clearly different 'positions' that can be held, which can be arranged in a developmental hierarchy of intellectual and cognitive development. Education and experience are likely to aid the 'journey' through these relevant 'positions'.

Since the initial work by William Perry, different theorists have defined and arranged these positions in slightly different ways. Essentially, however, they start with an initial position where learners view things as either right or wrong ('dualist'), and believe that there is a 'correct' answer to be found to any question (even if nobody knows it yet), move through positions that start to acknowledge uncertainty and see knowledge more as a matter of opinion, through, ultimately, to the view that some explanations, based on evidence, are more valid than others ('relativist').

Marcia B. Baxter-Magolda presented a four-stage model:

- Absolute knowing – the purpose of learning is to find and know the right answer
- Transitional knowledge – knowledge is partially certain/uncertain and the purpose of learning is to understand
- Independent knowing – knowledge is uncertain and the purpose of learning is to produce one's own perspectives
- Contextual knowing – knowledge is based on knowledge in context and the purpose of learning is to think though problems and integrate and apply knowledge

Her research with US students, at a well-funded, highly-selective institution, found that 68% of first year undergraduates were at the first of these levels and 32% were at the second; only 16% of seniors were at the third level, but this rose to 57% one year after graduation. One year after graduation the fourth level had still only been reached by

12%.

Implications for improving student learning

Arguably the most important thing that we can do is to make ourselves aware (as much as possible) of which of these stages our students are at, and then to offer learning opportunities to encourage and aid their transition to the next. Craig Nelson has offered a range of examples of how one might do this, including: considering the history of knowledge in a discipline (e.g. what was thought to be 'true' 100 years ago?), setting tasks such as having to choose between competing theories or ideas and justifying the choice, and hypothesis testing. A further suggestion he makes is "paradigm choice and paradigm mixing"; for example, considering the advantages and disadvantages of the different possible ways of addressing schizophrenia – "as a genetic defect, as a biochemical disequilibrium, or as a response to social stress" (p175).

Further reading

Baxter Magolda, M. B. (2004) *Making Their Own Way: Narratives for Transforming Higher Education to Promote Self-development,* Sterling, VA: Stylus Publishing

Nelson, C.E. 1999. On the persistence of unicorns: The tradeoff between content and critical thinking revisited. *In* B.A. Pescosolido and R. Aminzade, Eds., *The Social Worlds of Higher Education: Handbook for Teaching in a New Century,* Thousand Oaks, CA: Pine Forge Press

Perry, W. G., Jr. (1981) Cognitive and Ethical Growth: The Making of Meaning. In Arthur W. Chickering and Associates, *The Modern American College*, San Francisco: Jossey-Bass 76-116

Richardson, J.T.E. (2013) Epistemological development in higher education, *Educational Research Review*, accessed (1/9/20) at: http://www.sciencedirect.com/science/article/pii/S1747938X12000486

Learning is constrained by beliefs about learning

What do we know?

Linked closely to students' beliefs about knowledge (above), students' beliefs about learning have a significant affect on their conceptions of teaching and their approaches to studying. Again, different theorists have slightly different taxonomies, but Säljö[4] suggests the following five-stage model, which is accompanied by illustrations of how students holding each view might express it:

1. Learning as an increase in knowledge. The student will often see learning as something done to them by teachers rather than as something they do to, or for, themselves. *To gain some knowledge is learning ... We obviously want to learn more. I want to know as much as possible*
2. Learning as memorising. The student has an active role in memorising, but the information being memorised is not transformed in any way. *Learning is about getting it into your head. You've just got to keep writing it out and eventually it will go in.*
3. Learning as acquiring facts, or procedures which are to be used. What you learn is seen to include skills, algorithms, formulae which you apply which you will need in order to do things at a later date, but there is still no transformation of what is learnt by the learner. *Well it's about learning the thing so you can do it again when you are asked to, like in an exam.*
4. Learning as making sense. The student makes active attempts to abstract meaning in the process of learning. This may only involve academic tasks. *Learning is about trying to understand things so you can see what is going on. You've got to be able to explain things, not just remember them.*
5. Learning as understanding reality. Learning enables you to perceive the world differently. This has also been termed 'personally meaningful learning'. *When you have really learnt something you kind of see things you couldn't see before. Everything changes.*

---

[4] Säljö, R. (1979) *Learning in the learner's perspective: 1. Some common-sense conceptions.* Reports from the Institute of Education, No 76, University of Gothenburg

In this model, the first three stages can be grouped together under the heading 'reproductive' and the associated conception of teaching can be described as 'closed' – put simply, learning is seen to be passive and the expectation is that the teacher does all the work and makes all the decisions. The fourth and fifth levels can also be grouped, under the heading 'making sense' (or Säljö called it 'reconstructive'), with the associated conception of teaching as 'open' - where the learner is expected to do most of the work and make most of the decisions.

Implications for improving student learning

If we take a 'closed' approach to our teaching we are likely to reinforce a 'reproducing' conception of learning for many of our students, and dissatisfy the rest. On the other hand, there is evidence that students can become more sophisticated as learners as a consequence of their experience of more open-ended learning environments. Learning tasks and assessments that require more from the students (in terms of challenge, not amount) have been shown to be more likely to encourage a 'making sense' approach to their learning (see 'students learn by intention' below).

Further reading

Gibbs, G. (1992) *Improving the quality of student learning*, Bristol: TES

Learning is constrained by study skills

What do we know?

Irrespective of other contextual factors such as interest and motivation or ability (knowledge and skills) in the discipline, students' ability to learn is constrained by their study skills. The most fundamental study skill is arguably literacy and this is especially evident when students are working in a second or third language, but the skills required for academic writing, for example, may be a challenge for many native speakers too. Other essential skills would typically include: academic writing, numeracy, listening, note-taking, time management, IT skills, information literacy and research skills.

The other thing that is clear from the literature is that discrete, 'bolt-on' study skills courses intended to address any deficits in these areas are not very effective. Students are likely to lack motivation for them and transferability of skills learnt in this context to their mainstream study is likely to be limited.

Implications for improving student learning

Potential gaps or weaknesses in the students' study skills should be addressed through targeted skills development within the mainstream curriculum. Ideally, the teachers on a programme should get together and audit the skills required in their discipline and identify the units or modules in the programme, especially in the first year, where these skills will specifically be addressed and assessed – at least in terms of explicit feedback, if not necessarily in terms of marks. Where that is not possible, individual teachers should at least not take for granted that all students are sufficiently skilled in studying and should be prepared to readily offer support and guidance, as well as development opportunities. And these opportunities can be quite modest - for example, swapping notes and comparing those with the student next to you could be used as both a brief break in a lecture, and a useful way of enabling students to develop their note-taking skills.

Further reading

Gibbs, G (1981) *Teaching students to learn: a student-centred approach*, Milton Keynes: Open University

Fallows, S. & Steven, C. (Eds) (2000) *Integrating key skills in Higher Education: employability, transferable skills and learning for life*, London: Routledge

Students learn if they have motivation (intrinsic and extrinsic) and achievement goals

What do we know?

Students are more likely to learn if they are motivated to learn, and there are two sources of motivation – extrinsic and intrinsic.

With extrinsic motivation – the desire to achieve an external goal – the drivers may be short or long-term and may be positive or negative. Positive inducements come in the form of rewards – praise, the promise of being given a car, or a desire for a job with higher salary or status – while negative inducements come in the form of penalties and punishments – losing marks for late work, being 'shown-up', not being given a car, etc. The general conclusion from the literature is that extrinsic motivation is not as powerful as intrinsic motivation but, with regard to the classroom, probably the most effective form of extrinsic motivation is in the use of explicit goal-setting linked to mastery learning – i.e. that a concept or idea should be fully understood before moving on to the next learning objective (goal).

Intrinsic motivation – the desire to understand or learn for its own sake – can be related to, and influenced by, a number of factors and can be linked to taking a deep-approach to learning (see below).

Implications for improving student learning

Ideally, we want to encourage and stimulate intrinsic motivation in our students and this can be done in a number of ways. One of these is through self-regulation and providing students with the possibility of exercising choice. This could be choice of the topic to be explored and/or choice in exactly how the learning will be organised and/or choice in the way the outcomes of the learning will be presented and assessed. The use of individualised learning contracts[5] is one way of enabling and facilitating this level of choice.

Helping the students to be enthusiastic and interested in what it is they are learning (see 'the best teachers' below) is also likely to increase intrinsic motivation, and is likely to be linked to helping them see its relevance. Why is the topic important – to the wider discipline, to the world, and to them? Why should they want to know and understand it?

Further reading

Ames, C. & Archer, J. (1988) Achievement Goals in the Classroom: Students' Learning Strategies and Motivation Processes, *Journal of Educational Psychology,* Vol. 80, No. 3, 260-267

Nukpe, Philip (2012) *Motivation: theory and use in Higher Education*, Investigations in University Teaching Vol. 8 accessed 1/9/20 at: http://repository.londonmet.ac.uk/314/1/InvestigationsInUniversityTeachingAndLearning_v8_p11-17.pdf

Pintrich, P. R. (1999) The role of motivation in promoting and sustaining self-regulated learning, *International Journal of Educational Research, 31,* 459–470.

Richardson, J. T. E., & Remedios, R. (2013). Achievement goals, approaches to studying and academic attainment. In V. Donche, D. Gijbels, J. Vermunt, & J. T. E. Richardson (Eds.), *Learning patterns in higher education: Dimensions and research*. London: Routledge.

---

[5] see Anderson, G. et al (2004) *Learning Contracts: a Practical Guide*, London: RoutledgeFalmer

Students learn by doing, preferably linking theory & practice in a cyclical sequence

What do we know?

The literature is rich with evidence that learning can be substantially improved if students are active rather than passive participants in the process. Optimal conditions for learning include the provision of opportunities for students to interact with the information, ideas, materials, or procedures presented (see 'students learn by constructing meaning' below). A US survey of pre and post data for 62 introductory physics courses covering diverse student populations in high schools, colleges and universities found that when the traditionally taught courses (using little or no active engagement) were compared with those using interactive engagement methods, the latter were found to have an average learning gain almost two standard deviations higher[6].

Under the umbrella term, 'active learning', this approach was increasingly promoted in the 80s and 90s but has perhaps been subsumed more recently with the shift in emphasis to 'student engagement', which obviously encompasses far more.

A refinement of 'active learning' is to structure the activity as part of a learning cycle and probably the most widely known is David Kolb's experiential learning cycle:

---

[6] Hake, R *Interactive engagement vs traditional methods: A six-thousand student survey of mechanics test data for introductory physics courses*, University of Indiana, accessed 1/9/20 at: https://www1.physics.indiana.edu/~sdi/ajpv3i.pdf

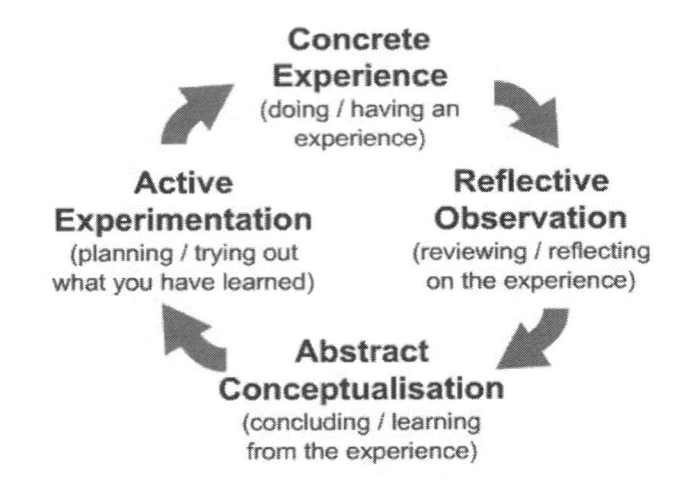

Concrete Experience
(doing / having an experience)

Reflective Observation
(reviewing / reflecting on the experience)

Abstract Conceptualisation
(concluding / learning from the experience)

Active Experimentation
(planning / trying out what you have learned)

The theory behind Kolb's cycle has a number of important elements. Despite the apparent emphasis on 'experience' in the name, it should be stressed that the cycle can be started at any stage. The cycle is also predicated on the argument that experience alone is not enough - once started, at whatever point, to be most effective, ideally the cycle should be completed at least once and preferably twice.

Implications for improving student learning

The message is clear that within logistical constraints, even in a single teaching session, time should be allocated, and activities designed, for students to actively engage with the subject matter. And whether activities are inside or outside the classroom (or a mixture of both), learning can be further enhanced if they are structured around Kolb's cycle. An increasingly popular way of changing the approach to teaching and to make learning more active, especially in the US, is the 'flipped classroom'. This has been defined as a "pedagogical approach in which direct instruction moves from the group learning space to the individual learning space, and the resulting group space is transformed into a dynamic, interactive learning environment where the educator guides students as they apply concepts and engage creatively in the subject matter" (The Flipped Learning Network, 2014).

The key features of the flipped classroom are that it changes the culture from the traditional teacher-centred model to a learner-centred approach, with in-class time providing greater learning opportunities and active exploration of topics in greater depth. Rather than the passive reception of knowledge in the lecture, subject content acquisition moves out of the classroom using multimedia resources – e.g. books, videos, podcasts, on-line learning - and possibly also structured group work activities. In the classroom, the role of faculty becomes even more important, guiding and facilitating activities, providing feedback, and possibly individually focused instruction.

Further reading

Freeman, S., Eddy, S.L., McDonough, M., Smith, M.K., Okorafor, N., Jordt, H., and Wenderoth, M.P., (2014). Active learning increases student performance in science, engineering, and mathematics. *Proceedings of the National Academy of Sciences (PNAS),* 111 (23), 8410-8415.

Gibbs, G. (1988) *Learning by Doing*, e-book available free at:
https://shop.brookes.ac.uk/product-catalogue/oxford-centre-for-staff-learning-development/books-publications/ebooks/learning-by-doing-a-guide-to-teaching-and-learning-methods-by-graham-gibbs-ebook

Sutherland, T. & Bonwell, C.C. (2005) *Using Active Learning in College Classes: A Range of Options for Faculty*, San Francisco: Jossey-Bass

Wieman, C.E., (2017). *Improving How Universities Teach Science: Lessons from the Science Education Initiative*, Harvard University Press
https://www.hup.harvard.edu/catalog.php?isbn=9780674972070

Center for Teaching Innovation at Cornell University. (2017). Flipping the classroom. Accessed 1/9/20 at: https://teaching.cornell.edu/teaching-resources/designing-your-course/flipping-classroom .

Chen, F., Lui, A. M., & Martinelli, S. M. (2017). A systematic review of the effectiveness of flipped classrooms in medical education. *Medical Education, 51*(6), 585–597 Accessed 1/9/20 at: https://doi.org/10.1111/medu.13272

Students learn by constructing meaning

What do we know?

While it may be possible to transmit information, or basic <u>facts</u> (the times of the buses on a particular route, for example) simply by telling someone this cannot be done with knowledge (in the fullest sense of the word) or meaning. In order to learn new knowledge, learners need to process it in relation to what they already know. Meaning is created by the learner through the interplay of new information with their prior knowledge, understanding and concepts.

Implications for improving student learning

This theory is a major argument in support of 'active learning' (above). Passive receipt of new information, be it through sitting listening in a lecture or through reading a book is less likely to stimulate the necessary interplay between new and existing knowledge. Creating opportunities for 'exploratory talk' and active engagement with the material presented, encouraging students to discuss, debate, explore and even play with ideas will be far more effective in helping students to clarify their understanding, process new information and construct new meanings.

A further consideration is the need to help students make explicit their current beliefs and thinking in order to confront existing concepts that they already hold which may be wrong. There is strong research evidence that if this is not done, new information may be superficially 'learnt' and even successfully used in assessments of that learning, while the previously held 'wrong' concept actually prevails as their preferred understanding.[7]

---

[7] see, for example, "A Private Universe" accessed 1/9/20 at
https://www.learner.org/series/a-private-universe/1-a-private-universe/

Further reading

Bruner, J. (1986) *Actual minds, possible worlds,* Cambridge, MA: Harvard University Press

Bruner, J. (1990) *Acts of meaning,* Cambridge, MA: Harvard University Press

Piaget, J. (1950) *The Psychology of Intelligence*, New York: Routledge

Vygotsky, L. (1962) *Thought and language,* Cambridge, MA: MIT Press

Vygotsky, L. (1978) *Mind in society: the development of higher psychological processes,* Cambridge, MA: Harvard University Press

Students are likely to have preferred learning styles

What do we know?

This is a more contested theory. Proponents argue that most students have preferences in how they go about learning, but differ in how they categorise and describe these different approaches. These learning preferences can combine in different ways and that can be called a 'learning style'.

Probably the most widely known model is that developed by Kolb. Based on his experiential learning cycle (see above), it takes the four points of the cycle as possible preferences and then pairs them in different ways to identify the following four different learning styles:

1. Convergers (abstract conceptualization and active experimentation) They are good at practically applying ideas and using deductive reasoning to solve problems
2. Divergers (concrete experience and reflective observation)
   They are imaginative, coming up with ideas and seeing things from different perspectives
3. Assimilators (abstract conceptualization and reflective observation) They are capable of creating theoretical models by means of inductive reasoning

4. Accommodators (concrete experience and active experimentation) They are good at implementation and practical application

Another popular and widely used typology is VARK[8], developed by Neil Fleming:

1. Visual (possibly better described as 'graphicacy'; this refers to a preference for diagrammatic representation, charts, graphs, maps, etc – not photographs)
2. Auditory or Aural (preference for listening and speaking)
3. Read/write (preference for the written word, either read or written)
4. Kinaesthetic (preference for doing, experimenting and experiencing)

Some of the criticism regarding learning styles has been aimed at inappropriate ways of using the theory, such as trying to customise teaching to meet the individual preferences of learners. Other critics, most notably Coffield et al[9] in the UK, have written extensively about the 'lack of evidence' to support the theory, and especially the failure to demonstrate that knowledge of one's learning style improves learning, but the proponents counter by arguing that that is because these critics fail to provide an adequate definition of learning. When a student learns, it is very difficult to attribute that learning to any source or multiple sources. This is made more difficult by inadequate ways of even knowing whether learning has occurred. It is not surprising therefore that learning styles have little evidence of their worth but, as Donald Rumsfeld said, "Absence of evidence is not evidence of absence".

---

[8] see https://vark-learn.com/
[9] *Learning styles and pedagogy in post-16 learning: A systematic and critical review,* Frank Coffield, Institute of Education. University of London; David Moseley, University of Newcastle; Elaine Hall, University of Newcastle; Kathryn Ecclestone, University of Exeter; published by the Learning and Skills Research Centre, www.LSRC.ac.uk 2004, available at: http://www.leerbeleving.nl/wp-content/uploads/2011/09/learning-styles.pdf
See also Pasher, H. et al (2009) Learning Styles:Concepts and Evidence, *Psychological Science in the Public Interest,* 9 (3) 105 - 119

Implications for improving student learning

Neil Fleming argues that despite the critics there is evidence of reported benefit from learners. He further argues that while knowing one's learning style is not a sufficient reason for improved learning, he believes that it is a necessary precursor to understanding how one learns, which in itself may be an important step towards being able to improve one's learning. The metacognitive student-teacher or student-student discussion is worthy in itself. So the first implication is that it might benefit students to think about their learning styles and the preferences they embody. Regarding teaching, there is the further argument that while it would be impossible to cater for every learner's preferences all of the time, teaching in a variety of ways might benefit some students who otherwise would be disadvantaged. Since Donald Bligh's work, still valid from more than 50 years ago, there has been strong support for variety in teaching methods and Sternberg's example in the reference below is an insightful endorsement of that (see pp16-17).

Further reading

Sternberg R.J. (1997) *Thinking Styles,* Cambridge: Cambridge University Press.

Teaching for learning

In addition to the implications for teachers already identified above, we also know that "trained teachers are rated more highly by students, are more sophisticated in their thinking about teaching, and have students who take a more sophisticated approach to their studying."[10] There are also two further bodies of work that are worth identifying.

---

[10] Gibbs, G. (2012) *Implications of 'Dimensions of quality' in a market environment*, York: Higher Education Academy accessed 1/9/20 at:
https://www.heacademy.ac.uk/sites/default/files/resources/hea_dimensions_of_quality_2.pdf

The best teachers (as rated by students) are enthusiastic about what they teach, respect their students, and are effective in helping the latter find connections with the former.

What do we know?

Quite a lot of studies, mainly from the US, although they may use slightly different terminology, come to this same conclusion. While students may forgive a lot when it comes to teaching skills, or even (lack of) knowledge of the subject, they are far less likely to forgive lack of enthusiasm, and teachers who they consider treat them with indifference or hostility. And this is not just about what students like or prefer – the conclusions from the literature are that these differences in teacher behaviour have an impact – for good or ill – on the students, and ultimately that is likely to affect their learning.

Implications for improving student learning

The message is clear – be enthusiastic about what you are teaching (however boring you may find it, or however many times you may have taught it before) and show that you care about your students and their learning – the latter includes finding ways to connect the students with the subject matter. What will make it interesting for them? Why would they want to learn it? (see motivation above).

Further reading

Carson, B. H. (1999) Bad news in the service of good teaching: Students remember ineffective professors, *Journal on Excellence in College Teaching,* 10 (1), 91-105.

WHAT WE THINK WE KNOW....

There are (at least) 7 principles of good teaching practice

What do we know?

A large scale research study was led by Arthur Chickering and Zelda Gamson in 1986[11], aimed at providing a user-friendly guide to the kinds of teaching/learning activities most likely to improve learning outcomes, based on the known research literature at that time. They produced the following seven principles for good teaching:

Good practice....

- Encourages student-staff contact
- Encourages cooperation among students
- Encourages active learning
- Gives prompt feedback
- Emphasises time on task
- Communicates high expectations
- Respects diverse talents and ways of learning

Implications for improving student learning

These headings are reasonably self-explanatory, and most are covered elsewhere within the theory summaries. However, perhaps especially for the UK, it is worth highlighting two of the imperatives: to emphasise time on task and to communicate high expectations. All the evidence is that if we have low expectations of our students, they will happily live down to them. Several reports have highlighted that, while identifying disciplinary and institutional differences, on average UK students spend fewer hours on their studies, in total, when compared with other European students. But at the same time, the UK has a very high percentage pass rate. It is hard not to deduce from these

---

[11] Chickering, A.W., & Gamson, Z.F. (1987). Seven principles for good practice in undergraduate education. *AAHE Bulletin, 39* (7): 3-7.

facts that, in many cases, the work UK students are currently being set is not sufficiently demanding or challenging.

Further reading

Enhancing Student learning: 7 principles of good practice accessed 1/9/20 at: https://crlt.umich.edu/gsis/p4_6

Washington Center News (1987) *Elaboration of the 7 principles* accessed at: https://www.lonestar.edu/multimedia/SevenPrinciples.pdf

Brains can be 'rewired' to improve learning

What do we know?

The brain does not simply record information as it arrives. Instead, the brain reorganizes information for more efficient recall and later use. The structure of information in the brain is one of the primary features that distinguishes "novices" from "experts." In the past 20 years, there has been an explosion of studies showing just how adaptable and malleable the human brain is and the previously held belief that the structure of the human brain does not change much after infancy is wrong.

Principles for remodeling of the brain to take place, include:
- Change is mainly limited to situations it is in the mood for
- The harder you try and more motivated you are the greater the change
- What actually changes in the brain are the strengths of the connections of neurons that are engaged together, moment by moment, in time
- Initial changes are temporary
- The brain is changed by internal mental rehearsal in precisely the same ways as achieved through interactions with the external world
- Memory guides and controls most learning

- Brain plasticity is a two-way street; it is just as easy to generate negative changes as it is positive ones

(Merzenich, 2013)

Implications for improving student learning

This new knowledge regarding brain development and learning implies new responsibilities to continually "exercise" and nurture the brain. Educational institutions and teachers are faced with the responsibility of designing curricula and learning experiences that will motivate, stimulate and guide positive 're-wiring' in student brains, while obviously avoiding practices which may do the opposite. Meanwhile, students bear responsibility for nurturing and engaging their brains during this important developmental process. Identifying students' prior knowledge before proceeding can also be an especially helpful technique. One teacher found that 70% of what he was about to teach was already known by the students. He therefore focused the majority of available time on the 30%.[12] This leads nicely into the subject of course design.

Further reading

Merzenich, Michael (2013 2nd Ed) *Soft Wired: how the new science of brain plasticity can change your life*, Parnassus Publishing

Zull, James Ellwood (2002) *The Art of Changing the Brain: Enriching the Practice of Teaching by Exploring the Biology of Learning*, Sterling, VA: Stylus Publishing

---

[12] Wratten, S.D. & Hodge, S. (1999) The use and value of prior knowledge assessments in ecology curriculum design, *Journal of Biological Education,* 33 (4), 201-203

Designing courses for learning

In addition to what it is possible for individual teachers to achieve there is also evidence that designing courses in certain ways can also increase the chances of improving student learning. One such idea we have seen already (above) is the possibility of designing a course around the experiential learning cycle. Here are some further theories that we should consider when designing courses.

Students learn by intention, which is affected by context

What do we know?

Students may adopt different approaches to their learning dependent on their intentions – what outcomes do they want from their learning. The literature identifies three different possible approaches:

1. Surface or reproducing *approach* to learning – the student does not seek to understand, merely to do what is required by the course to pass, which often includes a tendency to rely on memorisation.
2. Deep or meaning *approach* to learning – the student seeks to relate and reinterpret knowledge, with a desire to understand.
3. Achieving or strategic *approach* to learning – the student's primary desire is to excel and achieve top grades, which may or may not involve increasing their understanding depending on the nature and validity of the assessment tasks on the course.

A key aspect of this theory is that these approaches are not the same as abilities and the same student may choose to adopt different approaches on different courses, and in different contexts. Some of the reasons a student might adopt a surface approach may be personal – e.g. other pressures on their time, disinterest in the subject being studied - and might include lack of prerequisite knowledge. A strong influence on the approach taken is the context and nature of the course itself.

Implications for improving student learning

In some cases, whatever the teacher does may be insufficient to prevent a student from choosing to take a surface approach to their learning because of the pressures from their personal context. The student's beliefs about, and conceptions of, learning and teaching, and their stage of cognitive development (see above) may also strongly affect the approach taken. However, the evidence is that there are certain course characteristics that are more likely to encourage students to take a surface or strategic approach, and others that are more likely to encourage a deep approach.

More students are increasingly likely to take a surface approach the more the following characteristics apply to a course:

- An over heavy workload
- Relatively high class contact hours
- An excessive amount of course material
  (the combination of these first three making it increasingly impossible for the student to find enough time for reflection and assimilation)
- A lack of opportunity to pursue subjects in depth
- A lack of choice over subjects and a lack of choice over the method of study
  (the combination of these two making it less likely that the student is going to be interested or motivated)
- An over threatening and anxiety provoking assessment system

While the following characteristics are more likely to encourage more of the students to take a deep approach:
- The engendering of intrinsic motivation in the students; students wanting and needing to know
- Learner activity
- Interaction with others
- A well structured knowledge base - i.e. where content is taught in integrated wholes and where knowledge is required to be related to other knowledge

Further reading

Marton, F., Hounsell, D. and Entwistle, N. (Eds.) (1984) *The Experience of Learning*, Edinburgh: Scottish Academic Press (Especially Chapter 3: Marton, F. and Säljö, R. *Approaches to Learning*) 2nd Edition (1997) accessed 1/9/20 at: http://www.docs.hss.ed.ac.uk/iad/Learning_teaching/Academic_teaching/Resources/Experience_of_learning/EoLChapter3.pdf

Less is more[13]

What do we know?

This applies to both individual teaching sessions and the overall design of the course. It is an understandable concern of faculty that they have to make sure they 'cover' everything and to pack both their course and their sessions with as much content as possible. There is of course no guarantee that the students will actually learn it and in fact we know from the final assessments that the reality is that they do not learn everything. And the research evidence to support this has been there and known for a considerable time.

In terms of the classroom, one powerful US study[14] compared lectures in which 90% v 70% v 50% of the lecturer's sentences disseminated new information (the remaining time in each case being used for restating, highlighting significance, giving more examples, and relating the material to the students' prior experience). It found that students given the lower level of new content learned more and retained the lecture information better.

Another study in the Netherlands[15] showed that, to a large extent, class contact hours

---

[13] Craig Nelson, National Teaching & Learning Forum Newsletter, May 2001, Vol. 10, No. 4
[14] Russell, I.J. et al, 1984, Effects of lecture information density on medical student achievement, Journal of Medical Education 59: 881-889
[15] Gibbs, G, 2013 Teaching Intelligence: contact hours & student engagement, *Times Higher Education*, March 14th accessed 1/9/20 at: https://www.timeshighereducation.com/news/teaching-

have an inverse relationship with study hours: if there is more teaching, students tend to simply study less, making up similar weekly totals regardless of the ratio between the two. So increasing the amount of teaching can be counterproductive – or at least a zero sum game, achieving nothing.

Regarding the amount of content in courses, a study in the US[16] compared content intensive 'Major' courses with more concept focused 'Non-majors' courses, testing what the students had learnt, and concluded: "The most surprising, in fact shocking, result...was that majors completing their course did not perform significantly better than the corresponding cohort of non-majors."

Implications for improving student learning

These would seem clear. The temptation to cram as much content as possible into our teaching must be resisted at all costs and we must be realistic in terms of what it is reasonable to expect the students are capable of learning in the time available.

Further reading

In teaching, less is more. Small Pond Science accessed 1/9/20 at: https://smallpondscience.com/2017/01/23/in-teaching-less-is-more/

---

intelligence-contact-hours-and-student-engagement/2002432.article
[16] Sundberg and Dini, 1993, Science Majors vs. Nonmajors Is There a Difference, Journal of Science Teaching, Mar/Apr: 299-304

Assessment is a very powerful context that can affect intentions

What do we know?

For many students, assessment is the most powerful 'driver' and can significantly influence their learning behaviour, for good or bad. For example, an assessment regime that is heavily dependent on end-of-course exams, where it is relatively easy to predict the questions and model answers can be learnt by rote is likely to encourage undesirable learning behaviours. There is little incentive to study until the end of the course, or to consider the breadth of the subject matter covered, and even the possibility of cheating by using an answer created by someone else. And the assessment fails to reliably assess whether the material is actually understood, or the skills of the student developed (other than the ability to memorise). On the other hand, a course where various tasks are required as the course progresses, compiled into a portfolio which can be taken into the exam room where new material (e.g. new data, or a new scenario) is also provided and the student has to undertake a unique task, based on the new material (but relating it to and selecting from their portfolio), is likely to encourage greater time on task, breadth in the material studied – and act as a valid assessment of the students' knowledge and skills.

Feedback has the capacity to be the most significant and important part of the assessment cycle in terms of affecting further learning and student achievement; but unfortunately, current feedback practices are frequently judged by the students to be unhelpful and inadequate. In order for feedback to be effective, there are three requisite conditions – motive, opportunity and means.[17] The student needs to be *motivated* to engage with the feedback, and this is more likely if they can see they will have the *opportunity* to put the feedback into practice (and less likely if the feedback is accompanied by a mark/grade, which will become their main, and possibly only, focus of attention). They also need the *means* (help, support, guidance) to address their shortcomings.

---

[17] Shute, V. (2008) Focus on formative feedback, *Review of Educational Research*, 78 (1), 153-189

It has further been argued that feedback will be more effective if it is part of a systematic approach to bring the students into the community of assessment practice through the pro-active development of 'assessment literacy'. This should be done through engaging students in dialogue about assessment at every stage of the assessment cycle – through activities such as marking exercises, and self and peer-assessment. Teachers who demonstrate how they mark written assignments can also have a powerful effect on how students write later assignments. Providing students with exemplars of previous good work also helps.

Implications for improving student learning

Assessment has already featured in a number of the theories covered above, and is also considered in much greater detail in following chapters, but succinctly:

- It can focus the students' attention and ensure time on task
- It can set high expectations
- But if is too threatening and anxiety provoking it may have a negative effect
- Tasks can help to stimulate intrinsic motivation if they are interesting and can be seen to be relevant to the student (and possibly provide opportunities for student choice)
- Tasks can also challenge beliefs about learning and knowledge (e.g. the task of 'weighing up' two different paradigmatic viewpoints)

In addition, there needs to be an explicit intention to develop the skills of self and peer-assessment as graduate outcomes in their own right, through on-going dialogue and engagement in the assessment process, to develop the students from novice to expert within the community of assessment practice.

Further reading

Price, M. et al (2012) *Assessment Literacy: the foundation for improving student learning*, Oxford: OCSLD

Kirkwood, A. & Price, L. (2008) Assessment and student learning: a fundamental relationship and the role of information and communication technologies. *Open Learning: The Journal of Open and Distance Learning*, 23 (1), 5-16

There are certain "high impact" activities that significantly increase learning

What do we know?

What we know in this regard comes from a huge wealth of data gathered from the US National Survey of Student Engagement (NSSE[18]). Some of the headlines from that data are that high impact activities, i.e. ones which are most likely to have a positive effect on improving student learning include:

- demanding that students spend large amounts of time and effort on purposeful tasks
- a high degree of non-trivial interaction between both students and teachers, and between students[19]
- a higher likelihood that the students will experience diversity through interaction with others different from them
- Students receiving frequent feedback
- Students being presented with opportunities to integrate, synthesise and apply knowledge, and see the relevance of what they are learning

Implications for improving student learning

Courses that engage students in educational purposeful activities include in their learning design some or all of the following:

- Student opportunities to ask questions and discuss in class
- Student opportunities to make class presentations
- Students work together on projects, in or out of class
- Students receive prompt feedback – written and/or oral
- Students tutor each other

---

[18] see https://nsse.indiana.edu/nsse/about-nsse/index.html (accessed 1/9/20)

[19] This had already been identified by Astin, A. W. (1993) *What Matters in College: Four Critical Years Revisited*, San Francisco: Jossey-Bass

- Students provide each other with feedback
- Participation in a community-based project
- Opportunity for conversations with different races/ethnicities
- Conversation with others who have different beliefs/views/values

Further reading

Kuh, G. et al (2010) *Student Success in College: Creating Conditions That Matter,* Hoboken, NJ: John Wiley & Sons

Programmes where there is a clear & commonly held understanding of how courses are integrated, where staff and students "can see the whole picture," produce better learning

What do we know?

For students to learn effectively they need to see the connections between ideas and be able to link them to form meaningful 'wholes'. When it comes to course design, the coordinating ideas that underpin its content and structure, and may give it coherence to you, may not be obvious to the students – and this can be especially true on modular courses. The danger is that the students will not see beyond the detail of individual modules and not see the 'big picture' and therefore don't make the necessary, intended connections between ideas. In the worse case scenario, faculty teaching on the course may also not know or be aware of the rest of the programme and the intended 'big picture' or how their module or unit is intended to contribute to the whole. On the other hand, when faculty have a very clear idea and sense of common purpose regarding a particular programme there is evidence to suggest that the students perform significantly better.[20]

---

[20] Havnes, A. (2008), *There is a bigger story behind. An analysis of mark average variation across programmes.* European Association for Research into Learning and Instruction Assessment Conference, University of Northumbria.

Implications for improving student learning

Having an underpinning design behind the structure of a course is not sufficient to provide the necessary coherence to the students. The intended linkages and connections need to be fully understood by the faculty and made explicit to the students at every appropriate opportunity. This links to ideas below regarding positive learning environments

Further reading

Gibbs, G. (1992) *Improving the quality of student learning*, Bristol: TES

Gibbs, G. and Dunbar-Goddet, H. (2007) *The effects of programme assessment environments on student learning*, Oxford Learning Institute, Oxford: University of Oxford. Accessed 1/9/20 at: https://www.advance-he.ac.uk/knowledge-hub/effects-programme-assessment-environments-student-learning

O'Neill, G., Donnelly, R., & Fitzmaurice, M. (2014) Supporting Programme Teams to Develop Sequencing in Higher Education Curricula, *International Journal of Academic Development,* 19 (4) accessed 1/9/20 at https://arrow.tudublin.ie/ltcart/32/

Course design and activities built around threshold concepts and the use of concept inventories, can help students deal with "sticky" and "troublesome" knowledge

What do we know?

This comparatively recent theory argues that all disciplines have 'threshold' concepts – concepts that it is necessary to understand if one is to move on within the discipline and that are crucial to further understanding. (A common example often given is that of 'opportunity costs' in the discipline of economics.) These concepts are the ones likely to be found difficult and 'troublesome' by students because they challenge students' prior knowledge and require reconceptualisation. They are therefore the most likely places that students get 'stuck' in their learning, and the metaphor of 'a portal' has been used to describe them. Getting through them may be difficult and painful (what has been called a 'state of liminality') and once successfully passed through it would be difficult, and probably impossible, to return because the learner's views/beliefs/understandings have been so significantly changed.

Implications for improving student learning

In designing a programme of study it would be helpful to identify the key concepts, and which of those that would be seen as threshold concepts, and consider the logical structure of conceptual development of these in the course. Threshold concepts in particular will need sufficient time, and activities designed around them to help students through the 'state of liminality' in 'unlearning' previously held views and the acquisition of new understanding.

The development and use of concept inventories (a criterion referenced test designed to assess whether a student truly understands a set of concepts)[21] may help faculty to identify where the students are, both 'before' and 'after' given inputs and set tasks, and also to monitor general student progress regarding conceptual development through the programme. It is especially important to try and identify student misconceptions and, at the appropriate time, to help them, through carefully designed activities, to deconstruct them (e.g. see *A Private Universe*, referenced above).

Further reading

Land, R. et al (Eds) (2008) *Threshold Concepts within the Disciplines*, Rotterdam: Sense Publishers

Meyer, J.H.F. et al (Eds) (2010) *Threshold Concepts and Transformational Learning*, Rotterdam: Sense Publishers

---

[21] for some interesting examples in Biology at the University of British Columbia see
http://q4b.biology.ubc.ca/concept-inventories/

Sands, D. et al (2018) *Using concept inventories to measure understanding,* Higher Education Pedagogies, 3:1, 173-182, accessed 1/9/20 at
https://www.tandfonline.com/doi/full/10.1080/23752696.2018.1433546

Teaching practices need to be aligned with students' expectations

What do we know?

Thus far, I have focused on how teaching practices can influence student learning. But the students' expectations can influence how teachers go about teaching. Trigwell et al. described a situation (which they themselves had observed) in which tutors adapted their approach to teaching in response to requests from their students to go through problems using a more teacher-focused approach based on the transmission of information.[22]

The importance of aligning teaching practices with students' expectations was clearly demonstrated in a study by Mark Newman.[23] This attempted to evaluate the introduction of a course designed according to the principles of problem-based learning in the third year of a part-time nursing education programme. Up to that point, however, the programme had used a traditional subject-based curriculum.

---

[22] Trigwell, K., Prosser, M., & Waterhouse, F. (1999). Relations between teachers' approaches to teaching and students' approaches to learning. *Higher Education, 37,* 57–70.

[23] Newman, M. (2004). *Problem-based learning: An exploration of the method and evaluation of its effectiveness in a continuing nursing education programme.* London: Middlesex University. Retrieved from https://www.beteronderwijsnederland.nl/files/active/0/Newman%20Part%20II.pdf

also: [23] Utley, A. (2004, May 28). Problem method has high dropout. *The Times Higher Education Supplement,* p. 13. Retrieved from
http://www.timeshighereducation.co.uk/story.asp?sectioncode=26&storycode=188968

Moreover, the tutors who were employed to teach the problem-based component received minimal training and support. Perhaps unsurprisingly, the students were resistant to the new curriculum, and large numbers withdrew from the programme. As Newman himself remarked, problem-based learning "did not meet the students' normative expectations of teaching and learning" (p. 6). Elsewhere, he commented: "Students appeared to expect to be passive recipients of knowledge, taught to them by an expert, instead of having to make their own way through difficult material".

Implications for improving student learning

Although definitions of problem-based learning often imply that it encourages the development of more sophisticated conceptions of learning, it can also be argued that problem-based learning and other student-centred forms of course design actually presuppose more sophisticated conceptions of learning on the part of students. This might explain why some students have difficulty adapting to new forms of learning. Students who retain a reproductive conception of learning through exposure to a subject-based curriculum may have considerable difficulty adapting to the demands of a problem-based curriculum.[24] Changing students' conceptions of learning may therefore be a prerequisite for improving their learning itself.

Further reading

Van Rossum, E. J., & Hamer, R. (2010). *The meaning of learning and knowing*. Rotterdam: Sense Publishers.

---

[24] Richardson, J. T. E. (2013). Research issues in evaluating learning pattern development in higher education, *Studies in Educational Evaluation*, 39.1

Positive learning environments

Beyond the immediate level of the course experience, there is evidence that there are aspects of the wider, more general environment that can also be made more conducive to improving student learning.

Better learning is likely to happen in collaborative and highly interactive environments

What do we know?

Departmental cultures that create rich and engaging learning environments, that are collaborative and highly-interactive, where teaching is valued, and that engage in a processes to improve teaching are likely to produce better-performing students, even when compared with other departments in the same institution.[25]

This aligns closely with Wenger's conception of a 'community of practice' arguably going a long way to meeting his three key requirements of "a joint enterprise', 'mutual engagement' and ' a social entity', and with the notion of 'cognitive apprenticeship'. The latter takes a constructivist approach to learning where the context of the learning is all important – in this case that context being within a community of academic practice.

It is also possible to link with the previous two perspectives, a theory which started in nursing education. It sees the student as being on a learning journey from 'novice' to 'expert' moving, from the outside edge, ever further into the community of practice. The more successful department (and programme) will do all that it can to progress the student along that journey, and to bring them into the community.

---

[25] Gibbs, G. et al (2008) Disciplinary and contextually appropriate approaches to leadership of teaching in research-intensive academic departments in higher education, *Higher Education Quarterly,* 62 (4), 416–436.

Implications for improving student learning

To create an active, vibrant and welcoming sense of community, with numerous opportunities for both formal and informal interaction, and with the explicit notion of bringing the students into the community of academic practice.

Further reading

Wenger, E. (1998) *Communities of practice: learning, meaning and identity*, Cambridge, UK: Cambridge University Press

Benner, P. (1984) From Novice to Expert: Excellence and Power in Clinical Nursing Practice, Upper Saddle River, NJ: Prentice Hall

Physical learning environments affect how students learn

What do we know?

We know that a bad physical environment – e.g. cold, hot and stuffy, cramped, poor acoustics – will have a negative effect on student learning. But in the past decade there has also been a growing realisation that as learning approaches have been changing – e.g. increased use of media and technology, mixed-mode courses, blended learning, increased group-working – there is a requirement for the physical environment to also change.

Implications for improving student learning

The need for increasingly flexible learning spaces, ever-greater access to technology and especially web connectivity, and the need for social-learning spaces are probably the three main strands regarding the changes that are needed.

Further reading

JISC (2016) *Evaluating and designing learning spaces*, accessed 1/9/20 at:
https://www.jisc.ac.uk/guides/evaluating-and-designing-learning-spaces

And one possible tension

These claims about what we know about student learning are a personal view and undoubtedly would not gain unanimous support – and there are many arguments to be made about nuanced differences within many of these theories, and about the specifics of how they should affect practice. But arguably there is a high degree of homogeneity and overlap between these theories, and a significant amount of agreement in what they are saying, with perhaps at least one exception.

In the literature regarding the 'construction of meaning' there is a strong argument for the need for what has been called 'scaffolding' in supporting students' learning. And this has been linked to a concept developed by Vygotsky – zones of proximal development (ZPD). Put simply, the ZPD is the gap between what the learner can do without help and what they would be able to do if given help. Vygotsky, and many who have accepted this concept, believed that the role of education is to identify and focus on giving the learner experiences within their ZPD. Scaffolding refers to the help that the student needs and, as is implicit in the metaphor, can be taken away as the student's ability ('the building) progresses until the next ZPD when new scaffolding will be required.

But in the literature regarding 'threshold concepts', there are a number of aspects that would seem to be incompatible, or at least create serious tensions with the ZPD/scaffolding approach. Firstly, if understanding of a particular threshold concept is necessary for a student to progress it may not be possible to wait until they reach the appropriate ZPD. Secondly, the scaffolding theory is at least partially driven by a desire to make the learning process as painless as possible. But the threshold concepts theory would argue that the 'state of liminality' endured while grappling with a threshold concept and passing through that 'portal' will almost inevitably be a painful and difficult experience requiring, as it does, the loss of previously held understandings and beliefs.

The notion that all learning could be safe and relatively painless through scaffolded progression through successive ZPDs is an idealized impossibility but one that nonetheless is probably worth striving for. However, we also need to accept the reality that learning, and higher education in particular, should be transformative and that can be a painful experience. (This was also discussed by Perry – see above – in relation to the difficulties that students have negotiating their progress through the stages of cognitive development). And this may be especially true when it comes to the challenge presented by threshold concepts which probably requires even more scaffolding in support of the student at that time, in helping them deconstruct previously held views and to move through the state of 'liminality'.

Conclusion

Education is patently not an exact science. While the theories summarised above may be commonly accepted in the research literature, these ideas come with no guarantees. Every context and every individual student is different. The experience of higher education for the student will be an ever-changing collection of different combinations of factors and influences.

Teaching is a complex and dynamic activity that requires the teacher to make a multitude of decisions about goals, curriculum and strategies before, during and after each instructional episode. It is both intellectually and emotionally challenging and demands a high degree of involvement by the teacher. The often-frenetic pace of teaching does not leave much time to reflect, on the teaching-learning process. Thus, it is all too easy to fall into the trap of action without reflection.

It may be therefore be helpful to explore the gap between ourselves and our learners in the knowledge, skills and attitudes which we consider important in the subject we teach, and how we can help them reduce that gap as they move through their course of study.

The fundamental challenge for the scholarly teacher who wants to improve the learning of their students is to understand these theories, to know which to choose and how to apply them in their teaching, and especially how to adapt them to different contexts.

2 Purposes and principles of assessment

It is important to clarify some of the fundamental principles and issues which need to be applied to the design of any assessment strategies for any module or programme. For this purpose, let us define assessment as evaluation or appraisal; it is about making a judgment, identifying the strengths and weaknesses, the good and the bad, and the right and the wrong in some cases. It is more than simply giving marks or grades, although that may well be a part of it. And because it involves making a judgment it will almost always inevitably include an element of subjectivity by the assessor. However, we should strive to make assessment as objective, fair and transparent as possible.

Assessment plays a crucial role in the education process: it determines much of the work students undertake (possibly all in the case of the most strategic student), affects their approach to learning and, it can be argued, is an indication of which aspects of the course are valued most highly.

Purposes of assessment

It is easy to become so immersed in the job of teaching that we lose sight of the exact purpose of a particular element of assessment. There is then the possibility that we are not achieving that purpose, or that we overlook another form of assessment which might be more appropriate. We actually assess students for quite a range of different reasons - motivation, creating learning opportunities, to give feedback (to both students and staff), to grade, and as a quality assurance mechanism (both for internal and external systems). Because all too often we do not disentangle these functions of assessment, without having really thought it through assessments are frequently trying to do all these things, to varying degrees. In fact it is arguable that while it is desirable for assessments meeting the first three of these functions to be conducted as often as possible, the final two do not need to be done anywhere near so frequently; it is simply important that they are done somewhere. The implications of this are that while an essay question, where all the answers are double marked and the marks count towards the students' final grades, may fulfil all these functions, for all assessments to be this rigorous would be prohibitively expensive in staff time, while a peer-assessed seminar presentation, which does not count towards the students' final grades but is simply a course requirement, could fulfil the first three functions and may not even require a tutor to be present.

Formative v Summative assessment

This is the distinction between assessment which is mainly intended to help the student learn and assessment intended to identify how much has been learnt. Formative assessment is most useful part way through a course or module, and will involve giving the student feedback which they can use to improve their future performance. In practice, to varying degrees, most forms of assessment probably try to do both although the end of course exam where the only feedback received is a mark is almost totally summative. It is arguable that assessment in British higher education is too often focussed on the summative, and the accumulation of marks, coming at the end of courses, while students would benefit from more opportunities to build on their strengths and learn from their mistakes through the feedback from formative assessment activities staged throughout their course or module.

Assessment and course design

Assessment should be seen as an intrinsic part of the learning process rather than something that is just 'tacked on' at the end in order to get some marks. It should therefore be seen as a vital part of the initial design of the course or module. A model of course design can be described in the following three stages:

Stage 1: Decide on the intended learning outcomes. What should the students be able to do on completion of the course, and what underpinning knowledge and understanding will they need in order to do it, that they could not do when they started? (This obviously begs the questions what have they done before and what prior ability and knowledge can you expect?) These learning outcomes should each be described in terms of what the student will be able to do, using behavioural verbs, and described as specifically as possible. (Verbs like 'know' and 'understand' are not helpful because they are so general. Ask yourself, "What could the student do to show me that they know or understand?"). You may find it useful to group your outcomes under the following four headings: skills (disciplinary), skills (general), values and attitudes, underpinning knowledge and understanding.

Stage 2: Devise the assessment task/s. If you have written precise learning outcomes this should be easy because the assessment should be whether or not they can satisfactorily demonstrate achievement of the outcomes.

Stage 3: Devise the learning activities necessary (including formative assessment tasks) to enable the students to satisfactorily undertake the assessment task/s. These stages should be conducted iteratively, thereby informing each stage by the others and ensuring coherence

Principles of assessment

Reliability

If a particular assessment were totally reliable, assessors acting independently using the same criteria and mark scheme would come to exactly the same judgment about a given piece of work. In the interests of quality assurance, standards and fairness, whilst recognising that complete objectivity is impossible to achieve, when it comes to summative assessment it is a goal worth aiming for. To this end, what has been described as the 'connoisseur' approach to assessment (like a wine-taster or tea-blender of many years experience, not able to describe exactly what they are looking for but 'knowing it when they find it') is no longer acceptable. Explicitness in terms of learning outcomes and assessment criteria is vitally important in attempting to achieve reliability. They should be explicit to the students when the task is set, and where there are multiple markers they should be discussed, and preferably used on some sample cases prior to be using used 'for real'.

Validity

Just as important as reliability is the question of validity. Does the assessed task actually assess what you want it to? Just because an exam question includes the instruction 'analyse and evaluate' does not actually mean that the skills of analysis and evaluation are going to be assessed. They may be, if the student is presented with a case study scenario and data they have never seen before. But if they can answer perfectly adequately by regurgitating the notes they took from the lecture you gave on the subject then little more may be being assessed than the ability to memorise. There is an argument that all too often in British higher education we assess the things which are easy to assess, which tend to be basic factual knowledge and comprehension rather than the higher order objectives of analysis, synthesis and evaluation.

Relevance and transferability/Authentic assessment

There is much evidence that human beings do not find it easy to transfer skills from one context to another, and there is in fact a debate as to whether transferability is in itself a separate skill which needs to be taught and learnt. Whatever the outcome of that, the transfer of skills is certainly more likely to be successful when the contexts in which they are developed and used are similar. It is also true to say that academic assessment has traditionally been based on a fairly narrow range of tasks with arguably an emphasis on knowing rather than doing; it has therefore tended to develop a fairly narrow range of skills. For these two reasons, when devising an assessment task it is important that it both addresses the skills you want the student to develop and that as much as possible it puts them into a recognisable context with a sense of 'real purpose' behind why the task would be undertaken and a sense of a 'real audience', beyond the tutor, for whom the task would be done. Assessment tasks which replicates an activity that might be undertaken in the world outside the university (what has sometimes been referred to as a 'real world task', and the antithesis of an academic essay) can be described as authentic assessment – and there is evidence that authentic assessment can enhance student engagement and learning outcomes. (For more, see https://teaching.unsw.edu.au/authentic-assessment, accessed 1/9/20)

Criterion v Norm referenced assessment

In criterion-referenced assessment particular abilities, skills or behaviours are each specified as a criterion which must be reached. The driving test is the classic example of a criterion-referenced test. The examiner has a list of criteria each of which must be satisfactorily demonstrated in order to pass - completing a three-point turn without hitting either kerb for example. The important thing is that failure in one criterion cannot be compensated for by above average performance in others; neither can you fail despite meeting every criterion simply because everybody else that day surpassed the criteria and was better than you.

Norm-referenced assessment makes judgments on how well the individual did in relation to others who took the test. Often used in conjunction with this is the curve of 'normal distribution' which assumes that a few will do exceptionally well and a few will do badly and the majority will peak in the middle as average. Despite the fact that a cohort may not fit this assumption for any number of reasons (it may have been a poor intake, or a very good intake, they have been taught well, or badly, or in introductory courses in particular you may have half who have done it all before and half who are just starting the subject giving a bimodal distribution) there are even some assessment systems which require results to be manipulated to fit.

The logic of a model of course design built on learning outcomes is that the assessment should be criterion-referenced at least to the extent that sufficiently meeting each outcome becomes a 'threshold' minimum to passing the course. If grades and marks have to be generated, a more complex system than pass/fail can be devised by defining the criteria for each grade either holistically grade by grade, or grade by grade for each criterion (see below).

Writing and using assessment criteria

Assessment criteria describe how well a student has to be able to achieve the learning outcome, either in order to pass (in a simple pass/fail system) or in order to be awarded a particular grade; essentially they describe standards. Most importantly they need to be more than a set of headings. Use of theory, for example, is not, on its own, a criterion. Criteria about theory must describe what aspects of the use of theory are being looked for. You may value any one of the following: the students' ability to make an appropriate choice of theory to address a particular problem, or to give an accurate summary of that theory as it applies to the problem, or to apply it correctly, or imaginatively, or with originality, or to critique the theory, or to compare and contrast it with other theories. And remember, as soon as you have more than one assessment criterion you will also have to make decisions about their relative importance (or weighting).

Graded criteria are criteria related to a particular band of marks or honours classification or grade framework such as Pass, Merit, Distinction. If you write these, be very careful about the statement at the 'pass' level. Preferably start writing at this level and work upwards. The danger in starting from, e.g. first class honours, is that as you move downwards, the criteria become more and more negative. When drafted, ask yourself whether you would be happy for someone meeting the standard expressed for pass, or third class, to receive an award from your institution. Where possible, discuss draft assessment activities, and particularly criteria, with colleagues before issuing them.

Once decided, the criteria and weightings should be given to the students at the time the task is set, and preferably some time should be spent discussing and clarifying what they mean. Apart from the argument of fairness, this hopefully then gives the student a clear idea of the standard they should aim for and increases the chances they will produce a better piece of work (and hence have learnt what you wanted them to). And feedback to the student on the work produced should be explicitly in terms of the extent to which each criterion has been met.

Types of assessment

As has been argued already, the type of assessment chosen should be related to learning outcomes and governed by decisions about its purpose, validity and relevance. In addition, as it is probably true to say that every assessment method will place some students at a disadvantage to some extent, a range of types of assessment is desirable to hopefully reduce the element of disadvantage suffered by any particular student. Types of assessment to choose from include:

Essay

An answer to a question in the form of continuous, connected prose. The object of the essay should be to test the ability to discuss, evaluate, analyse, summarise and criticise. Two dangers with essays are that they are easy to plagiarise, and that undue weight is often given to factors such as style, handwriting and grammar.

Assignment

A learning task, undertaken by the student, allowing them to cover a fixed section of the curriculum, predominantly through independent study. Different methods of presenting the results can be used dependent on the nature of the task, and offer a wide range of opportunities for authenticity - a report (oral or written), a newspaper or magazine article, a taped 'radio programme, a video, a poster, a research bid, a book review, a contribution to a debate, etc. But it is vital to be clear in the assessment criteria how important the medium is, compared with the message. So if the product is a video how important is the quality of the lighting, the style of the editing, etc. compared with the content that is covered; if it's a newspaper article, does an appropriate journalistic style actually matter? And if such aspects of the medium are important then time must be given earlier in the course for these to be taught.

Individual project

An extended investigation carried out by an individual student into a topic agreed on by student and assessor. In many ways similar to an assignment, the main difference is the onus on the student to choose the particular focus and/or medium of presentation. As with any assessment where the product will vary significantly from student to student it is vital that the criteria are sufficiently well written to be fair when applied to different undertakings and results.

Group project or assignment

Where either an assignment or project is undertaken collectively by groups of students working collaboratively. This has the pragmatic advantage of potentially reducing the tutor's assessment workload and the educational advantage of helping to develop the students' teamworking skills. There are also some forms of product such as collaborative performance that can by definition only be achieved in a group. The major assessment problem is how to identify each individual's role and contribution and to reward it fairly. Solutions (none of which is problem free) tend to include combinations of: an individual component which can be individually assessed, tutor observation, and involving the students in some self and/or peer assessment as the ones in the best position to judge.

Dissertation

Written presentation of results of an investigation or piece of research, normally taking the form of an extended essay being less rigorous in its style and layout requirements than a thesis. The content reflects the findings of the investigation. This has similar assessment problems to an individual project.

Examination

This can take a variety of different forms. The most common factors are that it is done under comparatively short, timed conditions and usually under observed conditions which ensures it is the student's own work (although there are examples of exams where students take the questions away). Major criticisms are that because of the comparatively short time allowed answers may inevitably be superficial and/or not all the learning outcomes may be assessed. They may also encourage the rote learning of potential model answers. This can be avoided if the focus of the tasks set is on the application of what has been learnt, presenting the student with a previously unseen context or scenario or set of data which they have to 'do' something with. Some of the most common variations of exams are:

'seen' where the questions to be answered are given at a pre-specified date beforehand. The intention is to reduce the need for 'question-spotting', to reduce the anxiety, and to increase the emphasis on learning.

'open-book' during the exam students have access to specified texts and/or their notes. the intention is to reduce the emphasis on memorising facts, to reduce anxiety and allows more demanding questions to be set.

'unseen' arguably makes the student revise the whole syllabus because anything may appear on the paper (although in practice may do the opposite as the student may 'question-spot' and gamble on certain topics coming up.

'MCQ' objective tests asking multiple choice questions (MCQ) where the student simply selects from a bank of potential answers. Easy to mark (can be done by a

machine or even administered on a computer) and can ensure students revise the complete syllabus but arguably difficult, if not impossible, to assess higher order skills. Writing good questions is however very difficult. If you can find an appropriate US textbook there will probably be a bank of questions which come with it on disk.

Viva

Possibly used in conjunction with any of the above methods, this involves the student having to answer questions orally. In a comparatively short space of time it is possible to ascertain both what the student knows and the depth of this understanding (and possibly the amount they contributed to a group project and the nature of that contribution).

Performance

In many cases, when it comes to practical outcomes, the only sensible way of really assessing whether an outcome has been learnt is through watching the student actually perform it - whether 'it' is literally a performance, as in the performing arts, or a nursing student taking a patient's bloodpressure. Because in such cases the assessed "product" is transient, for purposes of moderation and external validation you may need to find ways of recording the event (audio or video). Such recordings can also play a vital role in giving the student feedback.

Self and peer assessment

There is strong evidence that involving students in the assessment process can have very definite educational benefits. Not so much a type of assessment, like those already listed, this is something that can be done in conjunction with any type of assessment. The important aspect is that it involves the student in trying to apply the assessment criteria for themselves. This might include: a marking exercise on 'fictitious' or previous years' student work; the completion of a self-assessment sheet to be handed in with their work; 'marking' a peer's work and giving them feedback (which they can then possibly redraft before submission to the tutor); or really marking other students' work (i.e. allocating marks which actually count in some way) - a seminar presentation, for example, or a written product using a model answer. The evidence is that through trying to apply criteria, or mark using a model answer, the student gains much greater insight in to what is actually being required and subsequently their own work improves in the light of this. An additional benefit is that it may enable the students to be set more learning activities on which they will receive feedback which otherwise would not be.

3 What do we think we know about assessment: the international state of research on assessment & examinations in Higher Education

The original version of this chapter was presented as an invited paper to the Symposion zur Prufüngsforschung (Symposium on Assessment Research) at the University of Hamburg, Germany, on 20th August, 2013

Introduction

I feel I must start by qualifying the very ambitious reference to 'international' in the title I was given for the original paper, and point out that the research and publications that have primarily informed it are all from the English-speaking world, predominantly the UK, USA and Australia, with some additional references from Northern Europe. Given that it is not a book, but just a chapter in abook, and time and space are limited, it cannot even attempt to be comprehensive in its coverage. It is also very much a personal viewpoint, reflected through the choice of the literature selected. I should also make clear that I am using the term assessment to encompass all judgements made about the work of a student and/or their skills, abilities and progress, including the associated provision of feedback.

A key foundation of the literature is that assessment is vitally important because of the influence it has on the students' approach to learning, the two major influences succinctly summarized by Cohen-Schotanus (1999) as:

- The Cognitive aspects of learning - what is learnt, and how
- The Operant aspects of learning – when learning takes place, and how much

So if, for example, a course unit or module has only one major assessment, and that is a three hour examination at the very end of the course, that is likely to have the following effects on the students' approach to learning. They are unlikely to put in much serious study time early in the course. If the exam is structured in sections that don't all have to be covered, this may encourage certain aspects of the curriculum to be ignored. When the students do start to revise for the exam, if by studying past papers from the course it is possible to 'question spot' (i.e. predict with some certainty what topics are likely to appear on the paper) then only a small number of topics will be revised, how few dependant on how big a risk-taker the student is and how confident they are in their ability to predict. The latter may have been helped if the teacher on the course has emphasised in certain lectures that certain topics are 'particularly important', which can be seen as code for 'this is in the exam'. And depending on the nature of the questions asked in the exam, the students' approach to their learning may well tend to short-term memorisation (Miller & Parlett, 1974). None of these behaviours described are likely to be ones that any teacher would want to encourage, but that is exactly what the assessment chosen for this course is likely to do.

And it is important to note, as David Boud in Australia has pointed out, *"Students can, with difficulty, escape from the effects of poor teaching,* [but] *they cannot (by definition if they want to graduate) escape the effects of poor assessment."* He goes on to argue, *Assessment acts as a mechanism to control students that is far more pervasive and insidious than most staff would be prepared to acknowledge. It appears to conceal the deficiencies of teaching as much as it does to promote learning. If, as teachers, we want to exert maximum leverage over change in higher education we must confront the ways in which assessment tends to undermine learning."* (Boud, 1995, p35)

Worryingly, given the importance of assessment in influencing student learning, there is a considerable, and growing amount of literature that suggests it is currently being done very badly.

In the UK, the Teaching Quality Assessment Subject Review scheme, administered by the Quality Assurance Agency during the 1990s, involved panels of peers from other universities visiting and reviewing the quality of teaching in a given subject in each institution. Regardless of the overall quality-judgment made, the aspects most consistently criticised across institutions, and across the range of subject disciplines, were assessment and feedback (QAA, 2003). And since 2005, the National Student Survey (see http://www.thestudentsurvey.com) has continued to reflect a similar picture with assessment and feedback being the aspects of their courses which students are consistently least satisfied with.

In the US, in just the three years from 2010 to 2012, there were the following four publications: *Higher Education?: How Colleges Are Wasting Our Money and Failing Our Kids - and What We Can Do About It* (Hacker & Dreifus, 2010); Arum and Roksa's book *Academically Adrift (2011)*; *College: What It Was, Is, and Should Be* (Delbanco, 2012); and Keeling and Hersh's *We're Losing Our Minds: Rethinking American Higher Education (*2012). While in Canada, Cote and Allahar published *Lowering Higher Education* (2011). All five books make similar, damning assertions about the declining quality of the student experience and the outcomes of higher education.

A second possible duality, when considering assessment, is in its two major purposes:

>assessment *of* learning (summative):
>
>>measuring what, and how much, has been learnt; differentiating between students; gate-keeping; accreditation; qualification; license to practice
>
>assessment *for* learning (formative):
>
>>this is more experiential; learning from mistakes; diagnostic; identifying strengths and weaknesses; providing feedback/feed-forward

And the arguments in the literature would suggest that we are failing in both these purposes in a variety of ways, including:

>Summatively:
>
>>(Un) reliability - locally and nationally.
>>
>>>There is growing concern about the lack of any consistency in standards, both across institutions and between different subject disciplines.
>>
>>Unscholarly practices in marking.

I would argue (and have - Rust, 2011) that university assessment procedures involve assumptions and calculations that a first year statistics student would be failed for.

Declining standards & 'dumbing down'.

This is a very common accusation, and there is certainly some evidence to support the argument of low standards. Whether, in fact, they were ever actually any better may be more debateable.

(In)validity.

There is a serious question as to whether we are actually assessing the knowledge, skills and abilities that we would claim that we are assessing. This may have been exacerbated by moves to modularity and the unitisation of programmes of study. In modular courses in particular, the design of the programme, and especially how it is assessed, may leave questions as to whether the whole (i.e. what it is claimed someone graduating form that programme of study should be able to know and do) may not actually be the sum of the parts (i.e. the combination of the results of the different individual module assessment).

Formatively:

Too much summative and not enough formative assessment.

Possibly another bi-product of modularity, it is arguable that most programmes have far more summative assessment than is actually needed to make accreditation decisions and not enough formative assessment to provide useful and effective feedback (Jessop et al, 2012)

Programme design.

Bad course and assessment design may encourage inappropriate learning behaviours, as has already been discussed. In addition, if there is a lack of clear and explicit linkage between the various parts of a programme of study, and a lack of opportunities for learning to be integrated, including in the assessment tasks set, then students are less likely to make the linkages themselves and much more likely to compartmentalise their learning, thus gaining less from it.

This paper will consider the evidence for each of these accusations in a little more detail, and conclude with what has been suggested as the possible solutions to these problems.

(Un)reliability of assessment

There has been research evidence that the marking of student work is not very reliable for many years. A study by Hartog & Rhodes in 1935 found that even with experienced examiners, 45% marked differently to the original marker. Possibly even more worrying, when asked later to remark the work 43% gave a different mark to the one they themselves had originally given. And there is no reason to believe that the situation has improved. Similar findings have been demonstrated by Laming (1990), Newstead & Dennis (1994) and, as recently as 2004, Hanlon et al found that 'careful and reasonable markers' given the same guidance and the same script could still produce differing grades. And, echoing Hartog and Rhodes, after a gap of time there was a difference between the marks given by the same examiners for the same piece of work.

Unscholarly practices in marking

The problems with reliability are perhaps not quite so surprising if we look more closely at aspects of the marking process.

Firstly, most processes are based on an assumption that it is possible to distinguish the quality of work to a precision that is not humanly possible (Miller, 1956; Elander & Hardman 2002). Whether in the UK, and a number of other countries that tend to use percentage marking requiring a precision of differences of one hundreth (although in practice the range in arts and humanities subjects especially is more likely to be between 35%-75%, but that still requires judgments with a precision to one fourtieth of difference), or in the US where I am told it is rare in many courses to find a mark below 70, which means effectively a 30 point scale, or in Germany with 10 gradations of pass, these are all levels of precision in differentiation that are not humanly possible – even for just one criterion. But most pieces of work are judged against a number of criteria, which compounds the problem still further.

This use of numbers, and their subsequent combination and aggregation also has serious implications for the validity of the assessment. *"What does a score of 55%, for example (an average to low mark in the UK), actually mean? Two students can have the same score while having very different strengths and weaknesses. The number ignores and obscures this detail………. Aggregation of criteria is a further problem. If one criterion is inadequately met can that be mitigated by another criterion being met well? And could a student go on failing to meet that criterion but always manage to pass because the aggregated mark is a pass?"* (Rust, 2011 p2)

Once the individual student's marks have been arrived at, there may then be either an informal or formal expectation that they should fit a so-called 'normal' distribution curve (bell shaped). Classes that don't may be subjected to increased scrutiny by the internal quality assurance procedures and in the worst cases there may even be a requirement for a mathematical adjustment to make them. But how can such expectations be justified? As Bloom pointed out, "The *normal curve is a distribution most appropriate to chance and random activity. Education is a purposeful activity and we seek to have students learn what we would teach. Therefore, if we are effective, the distribution of grades will be anything but a normal curve. In fact, a normal curve is evidence of our failure to teach"* (Bloom et al, 1981 pp 52-53*)*.

Once finally agreed, these individual marks may then be subjected to further abuses through their combination and aggregation with the student's marks for other pieces of work. This makes no sense either statistically (ignoring as it does differences in range and mean deviation) nor in terms of representing learning (Yorke, 2008), as it ignores the different knowledge, skills and understanding that the individual assessments were originally assessing (e.g. practical laboratory skills, oral presentation skills, analytical skills through a written report, etc.).

And even worse, as Royce Sadler in Australia points out, these numbers may also include marks for things that have nothing to do with learning at all. What he calls 'transactional and bestowed credits'; marks given for attendance or taken away for late submission of work, for example, where they are being used for behaviour control and/or modification purposes (Sadler, 2009).

The final distorting bad practice is that central university systems treat all marks the same regardless of the nature of the assessment task, or the subject discipline. Yet there is strong research evidence that students consistently score better on coursework tasks than in examinations and similarly in the more numerate disciplines such as mathematics and engineering compared with the arts and humanities or social sciences (Yorke, 1997; Yorke et al, 2000; Bridges et al, 2002; Simonite, 2003).

In addition, it has also been established that in the UK, given exactly the same set of assessment results, students at different institutions could end up with up to a degree classification difference simply due to the idiosyncrasies of the different institutions' algorithms (e.g. Woolf & Turner, 1997; Armstrong et al, 1998; Yorke et al, 2008)

Incomparability nationally

In the UK, the Quality Assurance Agency acknowledged in 2007 that, despite all their best efforts, due to the various distorting effects of different practices, when *"Focusing on the fairness of present degree classification arrangements and the extent to which they enable students' performance to be classified consistently within institutions and from institution to institution…."The class of an honours degree awarded…does not only reflect the academic achievements of that student. It also **reflects the marking practices inherent in the subject or subject studied, and the rule or rules authorised by that institution** [my emphasis] for determining the classification of an honours degree"* (pp 1-2).

For this reason, they then went on to admit that there was no possible national comparability *"…it cannot be assumed students graduating with the same classified degree from different institutions, having studied different subjects, will have achieved similar standards; it cannot be assumed students graduating with the same classified degree from a particular institutions, having studied different subjects, will have achieved similar standards; and it cannot be assumed students graduating with the same classified degree from different institutions, having studied the same subject, will have achieved similar standards"* (Ibid p2).

In the US this lack of comparability has also been unfavourably identified. "[There are] *few reliable measures of what students actually learn or are able to do because they attended a particular college"* (Hersh & Merrow, 2005 p3).

Declining standards

Despite this lack of effective comparability mechanisms, there has nevertheless been a considerable amount of evidence put forward to suggest that standards are declining. In the US, Hersh and Merrow claim *"Numerous reports in the last decade have pointed to a decline in the quality of undergraduate education"* and include the example of the Association of American Colleges and Universities three year study of 1000 institutions which concluded, *"undergraduate education … is significantly underperforming"* (2005, p1). And this has even been acknowledged by the US Department of Education, *"The quality of student learning at U.S. colleges and universities is inadequate, and in some cases, declining"* (2006, p3).

Other eminent critics have included Derek Bok, the former president of Harvard, who said that Colleges and universities *"accomplish far less than they should. Many seniors graduate without being able to write well enough to satisfy their employers. Many cannot reason clearly or perform competently in analyzing complex, non-technical problems, even though faculties rank critical thinking as the primary goal of a college education"* (2007, p7).

And based on their own large study, Arum and Roksa concluded that *"There are ample reasons to worry about the state of undergraduate learning in higher education" "…many contemporary college academic programs are not particularly rigorous or demanding" "they might graduate, but they are failing to develop the higher-order cognitive skills that it is widely assumed college students should master"* (2011, p2, p31, p121).

In the UK, it is harder to find quite such credible sources of criticism, but there is certainly no shortage of critics – obviously including the press, but also academics at Oxford University, employers of graduates, and graduates themselves:

> *"Oxford finals students [are] 'little better than school leavers' … some … show a 'distressing' grasp of their subjects and their answers in final exams are little better than A-level standard, academics have claimed,"* (The Daily Telegraph, 21 January 2012, p10).

> One in three companies believed that the [UK HE] education system was failing to equip young people with the skills required by British businesses, (The Daily Telegraph, 16 January 2012, p2).

> Nearly half of graduates admitted that their degree had failed to provide them with the right skills to enter the world of work (Ibid)

In addition, on both sides of the Atlantic, there have been repeated accusations of 'dumbing down' and grade inflation. In the UK, figures suggest that 66% of students gained either 1sts or 2.1s (the two highest grades) in 2012 compared with only 33% in 1997 (Thornes, 2012). In the US, *"In 'Grading in American Colleges and Universities'…. Stuart Rojstaczer … and Christopher Healy … illustrate that grade point averages have* risen nationally throughout most of the last five decades", USA Today (5th March, 2010). And in a study of 135 institutions published in 2012 found that 'A's currently represent 43% of all letter grades awarded (Rojstaczer & Healey, 2012).

In both the UK and the US there are also equally worrying statistics about a decline in the number of hours students spend studying. In the US, according to Babcock and Marks' 2011 study (cited in Arum & Roksa 2011, 3), the time spent on 'academic pursuits' (in and out of class combined) was 40 hours in the 1960s but only 27 hours today. In the UK, several recent studies comparing UK students with those in the rest of Europe found UK students at, or very near, the bottom in terms of the number of hours being studied per week – e.g. 34% students of UK students study 20 hours/week or less compared with 5%-25% in mainland Europe (HEPI, 2007) – and in the UK the semesters also tend to be shorter.

So what might be causing this claimed decline in standards? Well one suggestion, which has been argued very strongly in the U.S., is the unwritten existence of, what has been called, a 'disengagement compact'
or, alternatively, a 'non-aggression pact'. *"'I'll leave you alone if you leave me alone.' That is, I won't make you work too hard (read a lot, write a lot) so that I won't have to grade as many papers or explain why you are not performing well. The existence of this bargain is suggested by the fact that with a relatively low level of effort, many students get decent grades – Bs and sometimes better"* (Kuh, 2003 p28). *"A non-aggression pact exists between many faculty members and students… with each side agreeing not to impinge on the other. The glue that keeps the pact intact is grade inflation: easy As for merely acceptable work and Bs for mediocre"* (Hersh & Merrow, 2005 p4)

The (In)validity of much assessment

Whether or not the apparent decline is real, or merely a perception, could be questioned, as might whether standards were ever as high as we may like to believe, if we consider some older studies that raise fundamental questions about the validity of the assessment processes that we use.

When it comes to what students are actually learning, there are studies dating from the 1990s, in the sciences in particular, which suggest that students may appear successful, in that they are passing the necessary assessments, while actually not having learnt the fundamental underlying concepts. In 1992, Mary Nakhleh, at Purdue University in the US, showed that in a traditional chemistry course, half of the students who solved test problems could not explain the underlying concepts. At Harvard University, in 1998, Eric Mazur similarly found in pre-med physics that 40%, while doing well on conventional tests, could not actually answer conceptual questions. Camilla Rump, in 1999, at Denmark Technical University showed that, in mechanics, about half of the students did relatively well at the exam but relatively poorly in a test of their understanding. But Rump's paper went further in that it related the particular study to a range of other studies, from Scandinavia and beyond, dating as far back as 1978 (namely: Dahlgren, 1978; Johansson, 1981; Svensson, 1984; Pedersen, 1985; McDermott et al, 1987; Lybeck et al, 1988; Svensson et al, 1988; Renstrom et al, 1990; Bowden et al, 1992; Nakleh, 1992, Tornkvist et al, 1993, Prosser et al, 1996) with the bald conclusion that, *"The research shows concurrently that students often show serious lack of understanding of fundamental concepts despite the ability to pass examinations"* (Rump et al, 1999 p 299). And I know of no more recent literature that would provide any reason to believe that this situation has changed or is significantly different now. So rather than a picture of decline, there may actually have been significant problems in our teaching and assessment systems and practices for some considerable time – at least approaching four decades.

(Inter)national recognition of the need for change

As has already been shown, there has been criticism of assessment practices for some considerable time but recently there appears to have been some recognition of that criticism and growing concern about standards and the quality of the 'end-product' expressed at a national level.

In the UK, a government-sponsored report considering the UK system of degree classification came to the conclusion that it is *"..no longer fit for purpose. It* [degree classification] *cannot describe, and therefore does not do full justice to, the range of knowledge, skills, experience and attributes of a graduate in the 21st Century"* (Burgess Report, 2007, p5). And a Parliamentary Select Committee concluded that, *"It is unacceptable for the sector to be in receipt of departmental spending of £15 billion but be unable to answer a straightforward question about the relative standards of the degrees of students, which the taxpayer has paid for"* (IUSS committee, 2009).

The problem of a lack of comparable standards has also recently been recognised by the US Department of Education. " [There is] *no solid evidence, comparable across institutions, of how much students learn in colleges or whether they learn more at one college than another."* US Department of Education (2006, p14)

And in Australia, Dr Bob Birrell, the author of an influential study considering the standards of students graduating in Accountancy, stated, *"I regard the 2006-07 data as the best indication yet of the standards of Australian universities...they're nowhere near the standards required by the profession"* (Lane, 2009).

Achieving comparable standards requires the development of communities of practice

The UK's Quality Assurance Agency's belief in, and commitment to, quality assurance systems based on developing ever increasing levels of written 'explicitness' is somewhat surprising considering that a report by the Higher Education Quality Council in 1997 recognised that comparable standards can only be established through dialogue within a community of assessment practice.

> *"Consistent assessment decisions among assessors are the product of interactions over time, the internalisation of exemplars, and of inclusive networks. Written instructions, mark schemes and criteria, even when used with scrupulous care, cannot substitute for these"*
> (HEQC, 1997 para 4.7)

And the literature and research evidence is clear on this issue (e.g. Knight & Yorke, 2008); simply writing and sharing assessment criteria does not, and cannot, achieve common understanding and reliability in assessment. Criteria are socially constructed requiring the sharing of tacit knowledge over time (O'Donovan et al, 2004; Rust et al, 2005) and tacit knowledge is experience-based and can only be revealed through the sharing of experience – socialisation processes involving observation, imitation and practice (Nonaka, 1991)

"A social constructivist view of learning (Vygotsky, 1962, 1978; Bruner, 1986, 1990) argues that knowledge is shaped and evolves through increasing participation within different communities of practice (Cole, 1990; Scribner, 1985). Acquiring knowledge and understanding of assessment processes, criteria and standards needs the same kind of active engagement and participation as learning about anything else." (Rust et al, 2005 p232)

This can be seen as an ongoing cycle, with faculty engaging with each other in discussion about the assessment at key points in the assessment process: e.g. designing the assessment task and developing the criteria, discussing the meaning of the criteria, agreeing marking guidance to staff, and then moderating the marking – which should then feed into any future assessment.

Bringing students into the community of assessment practice

A very common thread in the research literature is that if we want students to understand the standards that we expect them to achieve, they also need to be brought into the community of assessment practice in the same way as faculty. After all, an indispensable condition for improvement in student learning is that *"the student comes to hold a concept of quality roughly similar to that held by the teacher"* (Sadler, 1989 p121).

Through student engagement in activities such as marking exercises, self-assessment, and peer-review, giving practice in the application of criteria and opportunities for discussion about interpretation of criteria, students can gain much better understanding of what the criteria mean and what the standards are that are expected of them (O'Donovan et al, 2004; Rust et al, 2005; Price et al, 2012).

And when it comes to feedback on assessed work, there is strong evidence that passive receipt of feedback has little if any effect on future performance (e.g. Fritz et al, 2000). Dialogue and participatory relationships are key elements of engaging students with assessment feedback (ESwAF FDTL, 2007) and essential if it is to be effective in improving subsequent performance.

Essentially, the argument is that students need to engage as interactive partners in a learning community, relinquishing the passive role of 'the instructed' within processes controlled by academic 'experts' (Gibbs et al, 2004), with a significant aim being to help the students develop their own assessment literacy, which has been defined by Price et al thus:

> "Assessment literacy encompasses:
> - an appreciation of assessment's relationship to learning;
> - a conceptual understanding of assessment (i.e. understanding of the basic principles of valid assessment and feedback practice, including the terminology used);
> - understanding of the nature, meaning and level of assessment criteria and standards;
> - skills in self- and peer assessment;
> - familiarity with technical approaches to assessment (i.e. familiarity with pertinent assessment and feedback skills, techniques, and methods, including their purpose and efficacy); and

- possession of the intellectual ability to select and apply appropriate approaches and techniques to assessed tasks (not only does one have the requisite skills, but one is also able to judge which skill to use when, for which task)" (Price et al, 2012 pp10-11)

The argument for the development of the students' assessment literacy also links to the increasingly important 'employability' agenda and the skills and abilities students will need beyond university. Assessment practices should also be *"about equipping students for the learning and assessing they will need to do **after** completing their course and the challenges they will face after graduation"* (Assessment Futures website homepage, University of Technology, Sydney, 2009).

At its simplest, I believe this literature and associated arguments can be reduced to the need for two fundamental conceptual shifts by faculty.

Firstly, the skills and abilities of self- and peer-assessment need to be seen as essential graduate attributes, i.e. they should be seen as learning outcomes in their own right, rather than just possible processes that might be chosen as ways of assessing the students. Once they are seen as vital outcomes this must inevitably change the approach taken to course design.

Secondly, in the words of David Nicol (2010), feedback needs to be seen as a dialogue rather than as a monologue (which is usually in writing). And he goes on to point out that a dialogue should involve more than two people (which technically is a duologue). He is not simply advocating a discussion between student and tutor but a much wider conversation involving students talking with other students too.

And these two conceptual shifts need to be brought together through the explicit intention of bringing students into the community of assessment practice. And the Holy Grail of what that community of practice should be like would be an integrated process where the two previously discussed cycles (staff and student) are intrinsically linked and constantly inform each other.

The problems of course structure and design

Atomisation and validity

Even when modules or course-units have explicit learning outcomes there are a range of concerns about the validity of the assessment process. Firstly, the assessment decision will be 'filtered' by assessment criteria, which may not have any direct connection to the learning outcomes (e.g. fluency, structure, referencing, etc.). This is likely to be compounded by the fact that one task may be expected to assess more than one learning outcome so the final decision will be an aggregation of the judgements about the different aspects being assessed. And then this overarching judgment is turned into a number and/or a grade which will be treated as 'credit' to be added to, and averaged with, other credit acquired from other modules but what does this accumulated credit actually represent? What validity does it actually have, especially regarding the espoused learning outcomes of the whole degree programme? Does such a system really assure that the programme outcomes have been met and assessed? In other words, does the sum of the parts actually add up to the espoused 'whole'?

The PASS project (a UK Higher Education Agency funded project led by the University of Bradford) has explored this question and has collected case-study examples of courses where explicit attempts have been made to overcome this problem and to ensure that the programme outcomes are being assessed (see https://www.bradford.ac.uk/pass/)

Slow learning, complex outcomes, & integration

A linked, and further problem in modular or 'unitised' courses especially, is a concern that because they are largely self-contained blocks of learning and frequently have to be 'delivered' and assessed in a relatively short period of time, they may predominantly focus on assessing relatively lower-order outcomes. In addition, concerns about reliability and cost may also tend to influence the assessment methods chosen and shift the focus of assessment away from the assessment of more complex or integrated learning. *"This quest for reliability tends to skew assessment towards the assessment of simple and unambiguous achievements, and considerations of cost add to the skew away from judgements of complex learning"* (Knight 2002, p278). The achievement of high-level learning requires integrated and coherent progression based on programme outcomes (Price et al, 2008).

It has also been argued that some kinds of learning just need longer, and that slowly learnt academic literacies require rehearsal and practice throughout a programme (Knight & Yorke, 2004). Ray Land makes a plea for the provision of *"Slow time ... necessary for certain kinds of intellectual and emotional experience, for the production of certain forms of thought, and for the generation of certain kinds of knowledge*" (Land 2008, p15, citing Eriksen).

Detailed course planning across a programme, including the planning of the assessments throughout the programme, is therefore essential if slow learning and coherent progression regarding the programme outcomes are to be properly and consistently supported.

Course design can encourage a surface approach to learning

Perhaps the most troubling aspect of the role of course design is that there is very strong evidence that it, and especially the choices made about assessment in the course, can result in encouraging the students to take a surface approach to their learning (Marton and Saljo, 1984).

The main course characteristics identified as being associated with a surface approach are:

- A heavy workload
- Relatively high class contact hours
- An excessive amount of course material
- A lack of opportunity to pursue subjects in depth
- A lack of choice over subjects and a lack of choice over the method of study
- A threatening and anxiety provoking assessment system

The more of these characteristics that apply to any given course, the more likely that students on the course will take a surface approach.

The actual type of assessment that is chosen can also have an effect on the approach students may take. *"The types of assessment we currently use do not promote conceptual understanding and do not encourage a deep approach to learning.........Our means of assessing* [students] *seems to do little to encourage them to adopt anything other than a strategic or mechanical approach to their studies"* (Newstead 2002, p3). And it is well documented that *"...students become more interested in the mark and less interested in the subject over the course of their studies"* (Newstead 2002, p2).

Possibly the most damning research finding of all, and one found repeatedly in many different studies from various parts of the world, is that what we currently do in higher education actually makes things worse. Students are more likely to take a deep approach to their learning when they start their course than they are towards the end. Many research findings indicate a declining use of deep and contextual approaches to study as students' progress through their degree programmes (Watkins & Hattie, 1985; Gow & Kember, 1990; McKay & Kember,1997; Richardson, 2000; Zhang & Watkins, 2001; Arum & Roksa, 2011).

And a fundamental reason for this decline would seem to be something in the very nature of the assessment process and the experience of being assessed. Dahlgren has recently shown that as soon as an assessment task is judged on anything but a pass/fail basis and even the simplest of grading systems introduced (e.g. pass/merit/distinction), students are more likely to take a surface approach and much less likely to see the task as a learning opportunity (Dahlgren, 2009).

Specific issues with 'traditional' examinations as an assessment method

Arguably there are possibly three reasons why you might choose an examination. The first, and best, is that it is the only way you can be totally sure that the work produced is the student's own work. But it should be noted that this is only true if the nature of the examination does not allow for 'question spotting' and the regurgitation of something that has been memorised. Dependant on the structure of the exam, if it does not have different sections to choose between, or lots of choice of questions, and it is not possible to 'question spot, it can also encourage the learning of a wide range of material. In addition, in such a case, if there is also a lengthy revision period prior to the exam, it may encourage the students to take a deep approach to their learning (Gibbs & Dunbar-Goddet, 2007).

However, against those three possible benefits there is a much longer list of potential disadvantages. There is the danger that what is assessed is primarily memorisation rather than understanding. If it is possible to 'question spot' then the student may be encouraged to limit what they bother to 'learn' and if there is a choice of questions that may result in only a limited number of the course's learning outcomes actually being assessed. Most examinations impose time pressures, which may affect some students more than others, and is the ability to demonstrate skills and understanding quickly actually important? This problem may also be compounded by the requirement for students to handwrite their answers – a practice otherwise almost completely alien to them as in the rest of their studies they are almost certainly writing everything with a keyboard. This may also adversely affect some students more than others.

A further negative is that if the revision time is short, as it is on many modular or unitised programmes, then it is likely to encourage the students to take a surface approach to their learning, going for short-term memorisation rather than understanding (Gibbs & Dunbar-Goddet, Ibid). And a final issue is that, for a variety of reasons, it is generally harder to give students feedback on exams than on other types of assessment task.

But there are alternative forms of exam...

The possible benefits of exams identified above may still be achieved and the disadvantages largely overcome if alternative forms of exam are chosen. 'Open book' examinations, where students are able to have access, usually to a limited range of reference materials, can reduce the inclination to memorise information and can also enable harder, more complex questions to be asked. But it should be recognised that more time may be needed.

Essentially, if understanding is to be assessed rather than memory, what is needed is a 'doing it' exam (Gibbs et al, 1994). An examination where the student is asked to perform, create, produce, or do something. Examples of this might include being asked to:
- comment on an article's theoretical perspective (humanities/soc/sc.)
- give advice to a teacher seen on a video (education)
- analyse the case notes and advise a client (law)

And in more practical disciplines there are more specialised and well established examples such as the Objective Structured Clinical Examination (OSCE) in medicine.

Oral examinations, such as a viva, have the added benefit suggested in the literature that students acknowledge there is 'no place to hide' and whether they truly understand will inevitably be exposed, consequently encouraging a deep approach to be taken in their prior learning (e.g. Sayce, 2007; Pearce and Lee, 2009) – but it may be harder to achieve reliability in oral assessment.

What is the solution?

So what is the solution to this multiplicity of problems with assessment identified in the research literature? In November 2006, international experts in the field of assessment were brought together in the UK and asked this very question and the result was the production of what they called a 'Manifesto for change' (download available at: https://www.brookes.ac.uk/WorkArea/DownloadAsset.aspx?id=2147552217).

WHAT WE THINK WE KNOW....

Subsequently, the UK Higher Education Agency brought together a further group of experts who, based on that Manifesto, identified the following six components as essential to the changes necessary to bring about significant improvement:

1. A greater emphasis on assessment for learning rather than assessment of learning
2. A move beyond systems focused on marks and grades towards the valid assessment of the achievement of intended programme outcomes
3. Limits to the extent that standards can be articulated explicitly must be recognised
4. A greater emphasis on assessment and feedback processes that actively engage both staff and students in dialogue about standards
5. Active engagement with assessment standards needs to be an integral and seamless part of course design and the learning process in order to allow students to develop their own, internalised, conceptions of standards and monitor and supervise their own learning
6. The establishment of appropriate forums for the development and sharing of standards within and between disciplinary and professional communities (HEA, 2012)

And in Australia there was a very similar, parallel development under the heading 'Australia 2020' which produced the following seven propositions for assessment reform:

Assessment has most effect when...

1. assessment is used to engage students in learning that is productive.
2. feedback is used to actively improve student learning
3. students and teachers become responsible partners in learning and assessment.
4. students are inducted into the assessment practices and cultures of higher education.
5. assessment for learning is placed at the centre of subject and program design.
6. assessment for learning is a focus for staff and institutional development.
7. assessment provides inclusive and trustworthy representation of student achievement. (Boud, D. and Associates, 2010)

As can be seen, there is a high degree of similarity and overlap between these two summaries of what is required. But it is important to note that these are not just lists to be selected from. They need to be seen as intrinsically linked and overlapping requirements, and treated holistically. There are no simple, 'quick fixes'; it is all or nothing. For change to be suitably transformative it will need to be fundamental and systemic, and to include the complete set of components/propositions identified.

Conclusion

There is a fairly high degree of consistency and homogeneity in the international research literature on assessment, both in terms of its criticisms of current practices and outcomes, and in the proposed solutions as to the changes necessary to put right the problems. And the need to do something appears to be gaining in recognition and perceived importance. So, despite the enormity of the culture-change needed, we may actually be close to approaching the point when the collective will to engage with the issues and the desire to bring about change reach a critical mass.

Acknowledgements

Thanks to Reinhard Bork for inviting me to write this paper, and also to Berry O'Donovan, Harvey Woolf and Mantz Yorke for their constructive comments on earlier drafts.

Bibliography

Armstrong, M., Clarkson, P. and Noble, M. (1998) *Modularity and credit frameworks: the NUCCAT survey and 1998 conference report,* Newcastle-upon-Tyne: Northern Universities Consortium for Credit Accumulation and Transfer.

Arum, R. and Roksa, J (2011) *Academically Adrift. Limited Learning on College Campuses,* Chicago: University of Chicago Press.

Babcock, P., and Marks, M. (2011) The Falling Time Cost of College: Evidence from Half a Century of Time Use Data, *Review of Economics and Statistics,* 93 (2), pp 468–47
Bloom B.S., Madaus, G.F. and Hastings, J.T. (1981) *Evaluation to improve learning*, New York: McGraw- Hill.

Boud, D. (1995) Assessment and learning: contradictory or complementary? In Knight, P. (Ed.) *Assessment for Learning in Higher Education*, London: Kogan Page, pp 35-48.

Boud, D and Associates (2010) *Assessment 2020: Seven propositions for assessment reform in higher education,* Sydney: Australian Learning and Teaching Council.

Bok, D. (2007) *Our Underachieving Colleges: A Candid Look At How Much Students Learn And Why They Should Be Learning More.* Princeton, N.J.: Princeton University Press.

Bridges, P., Cooper, A., Evanson, P., Haines, C., Jenkins, D., Scurry, D., Woolf, H. and Yorke, M (2002), 'Coursework marks high examination marks low: discuss', *Assessment and Evaluation in Higher Education,* 27 (1), pp 35-48.

Brown, S., Rust, C. and Gibbs, G. (1994) Strategies for diversifying assessment in Higher Education, Oxford: Oxford Centre for Staff and Learning Development

Bruner, J. (1986) *Actual minds, possible worlds,* Cambridge, MA: Harvard University Press.

Bruner, J. (1990) *Acts of meaning,* Cambridge, MA: Harvard University Press.

Burgess, R. (2007), *Beyond the Honours Degree Classification: Burgess Group Final Report*, London: Universities UK.
Cohen-Schotanus, J. (1999) Student assessment and examination rules, *Medical Teacher,* 21 (3), pp 318-321.

Cole, M. (1990) Cognitive development and formal schooling; the evidence from cross-cultural research, in Moll, L. (Ed.) *Vygotsky and education: instructional implications and applications of sociohistorical psychology* (Cambridge, MA: Cambridge University Press.

Côté, J., and Allahar, A. (2011) *Lowering Higher Education. The Rise of Corporate Universities and the Fall of Liberal Education,* Toronto: University of Toronto Press.

Dahlgren, L.O., Fejes, A, Abrandt-Dahlgren, M and Trowald, N. (2009) Grading systems, features of assessment and students' approaches to learning, *Teaching in Higher Education,* 14 (2) pp. 185-194.

Delbanco, A. (2012) *College: What It Was, Is, and Should Be.* Princeton: Princeton University Press.

ESwAF FDTL (2007), 'Final Report'. Available online at: https://mw.brookes.ac.uk/display/eswaf/Home.

Fritz, C.O., Morris, P.E., Bjork, R.A., Gelman, R. and Wickens, T.D. (2000) When further learning fails: stability and change following repeated presentation of text, *British Journal of Psychology*, 91, pp. 493-511.

Gibbs, G. and Dunbar-Goddet, H. (2007) *The effects of programme assessment environments on student learning*, Oxford Learning Institute, Oxford: University of Oxford. Accessed 1/9/20 at: https://www.advance-he.ac.uk/knowledge-hub/effects-programme-assessment-environments-student-learning

Gibbs, P., Angelides, P. and Michaelides, P. (2004), Preliminary thoughts on a praxis of higher education teaching, *Teaching in Higher Education,* 9, pp. 183-194.

Gow, L. & Kember, D. (1990). Does higher education promote independent learning? *Higher Education,* 19 (3), 307-3

Hacker, A., and Dreifus, C. (2010) *Higher Education?: How Colleges Are Wasting Our Money and Failing Our Kids - and What We Can Do About It?* New York: Times Books.

Elander, J. & Hardman, D. (2002) An application of judgment analysis to examination marking in psychology, *British Journal of Psychology*, 93, pp 303-328

Hanlon, J., Jefferson, M., Molan, M. and Mitchell, B (2004) *An examination of the incidence of 'error variation' in the grading of law assessments,* United Kingdom Centre for Legal Education, Retrieved from http://www.ukcle.ac.uk/projects/past-projects/mitchell/

Hartog, P. and Rhodes, E.C. (1935) *An examination of examination,* London: Macmillan.

Hersh, R.H., and Merrow, J. (2005) *Declining by Degrees. Higher Education at Risk*, New York: Palgrave Macmillan.

Higher Education Academy (2012) *A marked improvement*, York: HEA

Higher Education Policy Institute (2007) *The Academic Experience of Students in English Universities*, Oxford: HEPI.

Higher Education Quality Council (1997) *Assessment in higher education and the role of 'graduateness',* London: HEQC.

Hornes, J. (2012) External examiners and the continuing inflation of UK undergraduate geography degree results, *AREA*, 44 (2), pp 178 – 185.

House of Commons Innovation, Universities, Science and Skills Committee. (2009) *Students and Universities: Eleventh Report of Session 2008–09 Vol. 1.* London: The Stationery Office.

Jessop, T., McNab, N. and Gubby, L. (2012) Mind the gap: An analysis of how quality assurance processes influence programme assessment patterns, *Active Learning in Higher Education,* 13 (2), pp 143-154

Keeling, R.P., and Hersh, R.H. (2012) *We're Losing Our Minds: Rethinking American Higher Education.* New York: Palgrave Macmillan.

Knight, P. T. (2002), Summative assessment in higher education: practices in disarray, *Studies in Higher Education,* 27 (3), pp. 275–286.

Knight, P and Yorke, M (2004), *Learning, Curriculum and Employability in Higher Education*, London: Routledge.

Knight, P and Yorke, M (2008), Assessment close up: the limits of exquisite descriptions of achievement, *International Journal of Educational Research*, 47, pp175-183.

Laming, D. (1990) The reliability of a certain university examination, compared with the precision of absolute judgements. *Quarterly Journal of Experimental Psychology,* 42A, pp 239–254.

Land, R. (2008) Love, life and learning: responsible assessment for the 21st Century, in Rust, C. (Ed) *Improving Student Learning 15: Improving student learning - for what?* Oxford: Oxford Centre for Staff and Learning Development, pp 11-21.

Lane, B (2009) Degrees still lure low-skill migrants, *The Australian*, January 14th, 2009.

Marton, F. and Säljö, R. (1984) *Approaches to Learning,* in Marton, F., Hounsell, D. and Entwistle, N. (Eds.) *The Experience of Learning*, Edinburgh: Scottish Academic Press [2nd Edition (1997) accessed 1/9/20 at:
https://www.ed.ac.uk/institute-academic-development/learning-teaching/research/experience-of-learning

Mazur, E. (1998) Moving the Mountain: Impediments to Change, in Millar, S.B. (Ed) *Indicators of Success in Postsecondary SMET Education: Shapes of the Future. Synthesis and Proceedings of the Third Annual NISE Forum*, Madison, WI: Wisconsin Center for Education Research, pp 91-93.

McKay, J. and Kember, D (1997), Spoon feeding leads to regurgitation: a better diet can result in more digestible learning outcomes, *Higher Education Research & Development*, 16 (1), pp 55 – 67.

Miller, C.M.I. & Parlett, M. (1974) *Up to the Mark: a study of the examination game,* Guildford: Society for Research into Higher Education.

Miller, G.A. (1956) The magical number seven, plus or minus two: some limits on our capacity for processing information, *Psychological Review,* 63, pp 81–97.

Nakhleh, M. B. (1992) Why Some Students Don't Learn Chemistry, *Journal of Chemical Education* 69 (3), pp 191-196.

Newstead, S.E. (2002) Examining the examiners: why are we so bad at assessing students? *Psychology Learning and Teaching*, 2 (2), pp 70-75.

Newstead, S.E. & Dennis, I. (1994) Examiners examined: The reliability of exam marking in psychology, *The Psychologist,* 7, pp 216–219.

Nicol, D (2010) From monologue to dialogue: improving written feedback in mass higher education, *Assessment and Evaluation in Higher Education*, 35 (5), pp 501-517.

Nonaka, I. (1991) The knowledge-creating company, *The Harvard Business Review,* November-December, pp. 96-104.

O'Donovan, B., Price, M. & Rust, C. (2004) Know what I mean? Enhancing student understanding of assessment standards and criteria, *Teaching in Higher Education,* 9 (3), pp 145-158.

Pearce, G and Lee, G. (2009) Viva Voce (Oral Examination) as an Assessment Method. Insights From Marketing Students, *Journal of Marketing Education*, 31 (2), pp 120-130

Price, M., O'Donovan, B., Rust, C. & Carroll, J (2008) Assessment standards: a manifesto for change, *Brookes eJournal of Learning and Teaching*, 2 (3), 2008.

Price, M., Rust, C., O'Donovan, B., Handley, K. with Bryant, R. (2012) *Assessment literacy: the foundation for improving student learning*, Oxford: Oxford Centre for Staff and Learning Development

Quality Assurance Agency for Higher Education (2003) *Learning from Subject Review 1993-2001*, Gloucester: QAA

Quality Assurance Agency for Higher Education (2007). *The classification of degree awards, QAA Briefing Paper: Quality Matters.*

Richardson, J.T.E. (2000) *Researching Student Learning: Approaches to Studying in Campus-based and Distance Education*, Buckingham: SRHE and Open University Press

Rojstaczer, S. and Healy,C. (2012) Where A is ordinary: The evolution of American college and university grading, 1940–2009, *Teachers College Record,* 114 (7), pp 1-23.

Rump, C, Jacobsen, A and Clemmensen, T. (1999) Improving Conceptual Understanding Using Qualitative Tests, in Rust, C (Ed) *Improving student learning - 6 Improving student learning outcomes,* Oxford: Oxford Centre for Staff and Learning Development, pp 298-308.

Rust, C. (2011) The unscholarly use of numbers in our assessment practices; what will make us change? *International Journal for the Scholarship of Teaching and Learning,* 5 (1) Accessed 1/9/20 at: https://digitalcommons.georgiasouthern.edu/ij-sotl/vol5/iss1/4/

Rust, C., O'Donovan, B & Price, M. (2005) A social constructivist assessment process model: how the research literature shows us this could be best practice, *Assessment and Evaluation in Higher Education,* 30 (3), pp 233-241

Sadler, D. R. (1989) Formative assessment and the design of instructional systems, *Instructional Science*, 18, pp 119-144.

Sadler, D.R. (2009) Fidelity as a precondition for integrity in grading academic achievement, *Assessment and Evaluation in Higher Education*

Sayce, S. (2007) Managing the fear factor (or how a mini-viva assessment can improve the process of learning for international students), in Remenyi, D. (Ed) *Proceedings of the 6th European Conference on Research Methodology for Business and Management Studies,* Reading: Academic Conference Ltd, pp 275-282.

Scribner, S. (1985) Vygotsky's uses of history, in Wertsch, J. (Ed.) *Culture, communication and cognition: Vygotskian perspectives,* Cambridge, MA: Cambridge University Press, pp 119–145.

Simonite, V. (2003) The impact of coursework on degree classifications and the performance of individual students, Assessment and Evaluation in Higher Education, 28 (5), pp 459-470.

US Department of Education (2006) *A Test of Leadership: Charting the Future of US Higher Education*, Washington DC: US Dept. of Education.

Vygotsky, L. (1962) *Thought and language,* Cambridge, MA: MIT Press

Vygotsky, L. S. (1978), *Mind in society: the development of higher psychological processes*, MA: Harvard University Press.

Watkins, D., and Hattie, J. (1985) A longitudinal study of the approaches to learning of Australian tertiary students, *Human Learning*, 4, pp. 127-41.

Woolf, H. and Turner, D. (1997) Honours classifications: the need for transparency. *The New Academic,* Autumn, pp. 10–12.

Yorke, M. (1997) "Module mark distribution in eight subject areas and some issues they raise", in N. Jackson (Ed), *Modular higher education in the UK,* London: Higher Education Quality Council, pp 105-107

Yorke, M. (2008) *Grading student achievement in higher education: Signals and shortcom- ings.* Abingdon: Routledge.

Yorke, M., Bridges, P and Woolf, H. (2000), 'Mark distributions and marking practices in UK higher education; some challenging issues', *Active Learning in Higher Education,* 1 (1), pp. 7-27.

Yorke, M., H. Woolf, M. Stowell, R. Allen, C. Haines, M. Redding, D. Scurry, G. Taylor-Russell, W. Turnbull, and L. Walker. (2008) Enigmatic variations: Honours degree assessment regulations in the UK, *Higher Education Quarterly* 62 (3), pp 157–80.

Zhang, L. F. and Watkins, D. (2001) Cognitive development and student approaches to learning: an investigation of Perry's theory with Chinese and US university students, *Higher Education,* 41, 236-261.

4 Re-thinking assessment: a programme leader's guide

"A grade can be regarded only as an inadequate report of an inaccurate judgement by a biased and variable judge of the extent to which a student has attained an undefined level of mastery of an unknown proportion of an indefinite amount of material"

(Dressel, 1957 p6)

Despite this wonderful summary of the problems with assessment, distilled into just one sentence, sixty years later assessment practices that lack reliability and validity are the norm rather than the exception in universities across the sector and around the world. It is the intention of this chapter to offer guidance to anyone, but especially programme leaders and their teams, who wants to take a fresh look at their assessment practice, offering practical ideas based on the appropriate assessment literature.

Why this is important, can possibly best be summarised in the following observation by David Boud, *"Students can, with difficulty, escape from the effects of poor teaching, they cannot (by definition if they want to graduate) escape the effects of poor assessment"* (Boud, 1995 p35).

And as to what is actually wrong with many of our practices, a more detailed, and therefore more useful thesis than that offered by Dressel, can be found in the work of the PASS project in the UK, which argues that there are six common problems with the assessment of student programmes in universities today (programme meaning the combination of modules or units that comprise the total student course experience).

1. *Failure to ensure the assessment of the espoused programme outcomes.*
   Because students may have choices between modules and the route they take through the programme, and even if that is not the case, because assessment of module learning outcomes is often aggregated, so not all may have to be passed to pass the module, it can't be guaranteed that students graduating the programme have met all the stated module learning outcomes, let alone the programme outcomes.
2. *Atomisation of assessment: focused, at the micro-level, on what is easy to assess; failure to integrate and assess complex, higher-order learning; the sum of parts not making the intended whole.*
   Even if all module learning outcomes do have to be met in order to pass, for the above reasons, they may not actually add up to the espoused programme outcomes.
3. *Students and staff failing to see the links/coherence of the programme.*
   Even if the previous two issues have been satisfactorily addressed, and the module assessments do link together to ensure that learning from different modules is integrated, and the programme outcomes are met, do the faculty understand the linkages and structure of the programme? And even if they do now, will they after three or four years when there has been some turnover in the staffing? And even if faculty do understand, do they ensure that the linkages and structure are communicated to the students sufficiently that the students understand how the programme is intended to fit together?
4. *Modules are too short to focus and provide feedback on slowly learnt literacies and/or complex learning.*
   Modules can often be just a term or a semester long. Can every topic be reduced and taught in such short periods of time? What about weaker students who may need longer? What about more complex parts of the curriculum?
5. *Students and staff adopting a 'tick-box' mentality, focused on marks, engendering a surface approach to learning that can 'encourage' plagiarism and 'game-playing'.*
   Again, even if the module assessments do link together to ensure that learning from different modules is integrated and the programme outcomes are met, does the apparent compartmentalised structure of modularity coupled with the importance of the marks awarded and their effect on the student's final result for the programme, encourage a surface approach focussed on gaining marks rather than focussed on learning?

WHAT WE THINK WE KNOW....

6. *Too much summative assessment, leading to overworked staff, not enough formative assessment and inability to 'see the wood for the trees' in the accumulated results.*
   Compared with traditional, linear courses, modularity inevitably increases the amount of summative assessment. Each module has to be assessed, the argument goes, if it is to count – and very quickly one assessment is considered insufficient and it becomes two, or three or more. The challenge of assessing a range of diverse of learning outcomes is a major problem here. The purposes of summative assessment to make decisions on student progression, and ultimately whether they should pass and, in some cases, about fitness to practice, could be done with far fewer assessments, and probably more accurately. It is also arguable that with the increases in summative assessment caused by modularity, plus the significant increase in class and cohort size caused by the general 'massification' of higher education, the activity that staff have given up in order to cope is formative assessment. And formative assessment is vital in offering opportunities for students to undertake assessment tasks that don't count for marks where they can take risks and learn from their mistakes.

(From the PASS Project Position Paper – accessed 1/9/20 at:
https://www.bradford.ac.uk/pass/resources/position-paper.pdf

I would suggest that any programme leader, or Head of School/Department, who seriously wants to improve their assessment practice should start by a detailed consideration of these six general problems, and identifying the degree to which they apply and are issues on their particular programme/s.

As for the solutions, they can be summarised thus:

Less but better summative assessment

Summative assessment should explicitly link to learning outcomes, especially programme learning outcomes, and the assessment of integrated learning (what the PASS project called programme focussed assessment).

Reconsider how best to record summative assessment of learning outcomes and consider ways of moving to simple grading (e.g. pass/fail or pass/merit/distinction) as opposed to marks or percentages.

More formative assessment, and actively develop students' assessment literacy within a community of assessment practice

The rest of this chapter will consider each of these in more detail.

Programme-focussed assessment

Assessment should be **"specifically designed to address major programme outcomes** *rather than very specific or isolated components of the course. It follows then that such assessment* **is integrative in nature**, *trying to bring together understanding and skills in ways which represent key programme aims [**valid**]. As a result, the assessment is likely to be more* **authentic and meaningful** *[**relevant**] to students, staff and external stakeholders."*

[PASS Project Position Paper - my emphasis, and additions in brackets]

The first basic step in achieving this is for the programme team to ensure that it is designed according to Biggs' principle of 'constructive alignment' (Biggs, 1999). "The fundamental principle of constructive alignment is that a good teaching system aligns teaching method and assessment to the learning activities stated in the objectives so that all aspects of this system are in accord in supporting appropriate student learning" (Ibid). This principle seems to be widely accepted across much of the sector, but almost solely at the level of the module. It should also be noted that while Biggs refers to 'objectives', generally the sector has preferred to use the notion of 'outcomes', which is arguably more helpful.

WHAT WE THINK WE KNOW....

The concomitant three-stage design model - the essence of 'constructive alignment' - is:

1. Identify the "desired" outcomes?
2. Identify the appropriate teaching methods which are likely to require students to behave in ways that are likely to achieve those outcomes
3. Identify assessment tasks that will show if the outcomes achieved by the student match those that were intended or desired

Before considering individual modules, this approach needs to be applied first, at the level of the programme which, by necessity, means bringing the 'team' of module leaders together at this initial design stage, and starting with the identification of the desired programme learning outcomes – obviously taking account of professional body requirements, national subject benchmark statements, and the like, where appropriate. Often module leaders do not feel that they are part of a team, but if a programme is to be successful it needs to be seen by all involved as a team enterprise – and this initial meeting is vital to initiating that view. In addition to agreeing the programme outcomes, it is also helpful to further identify specific outcomes for each year of the programme – what would you expect a successful a student to know and be able to do by the end of their first year, second year, etc.?

Through the process of working to help programme teams take a programme-focussed approach to course design, a group of developers from Dublin Institute of Technology and University College Dublin identified the importance of what they call "curriculum sequencing" which, they argue, has three vital elements (O'Neill, Donnelly & Fitzmaurice, 2014):

1. Develop a collective philosophy – what do you want to be distinctive about your course and your graduates? What is the course designed to achieve? Why teach it in this particular way?
2. Communicate sequencing to students and staff – ensure that all staff teaching on the programme understand the relationships between modules and how the programme is meant to come together and be seen as an integrated 'whole' (which may well need to be repeated as staff change), and that this is then further communicated to the students.
3. Develop strong building blocks – which are very likely to be linked to ensuring the 'delivery' and assessment of the programme outcomes.

In relation to the first two elements, it is interesting to note that they are strongly supported by some work done by Anton Havnes some ten years ago. In a detailed study into what might explain the differences between programmes that had higher than average student results with other programmes in the same institution with below average outcomes the only clear significant difference he could find was the degree to which staff and students had a sense of how the modules fitted together and what the overall programme was trying to deliver. His conclusion was that where there is a greater sense of the holistic programme, students are likely to achieve higher standards than on more fragmented programmes (Havnes, 2008). While in the US, in their detailed consideration of the origins of underperformance in Higher Education in America (2015), Mascolo and Castillo argue that one of the main actions necessary to redress that underperformance is to move *"toward an integrated rather than fragmented curriculum"* (p25). This also chimes with analysis of the UK National Student Survey results that, "The single best predictor of 'Overall Satisfaction' was *"The course was well designed and running smoothly"*" (Langan et al, 2013), reconfirmed more recently by Burgess et al (2018).

And if gaining programme coherence cannot be achieved because it's a multidisciplinary programme, and staff cannot work together sufficiently (perhaps they're not geographically co-located, or are in very diverse disciplines) then at least they should make clear the differences between the different parts of the programme, and especially their different epistemic frameworks, and how this will be communicated to the students.

So far as the notion of 'strong building blocks' is concerned, it may be useful to consider the following three practical examples of what that might look like:

> 1. An Australian university has considered including in its assessment policy that all programmes must identify capstone and cornerstone (small capstones) modules – a capstone module being one that is explicitly intended to draw together and integrate, and assess that integration of, learning from preceding modules. There would be no prescription as to where or how many such modules there should be, just that the programme must have and identify them. This is a simple but incredibly innovative and useful idea.

2, A European Business School has a course structure for each semester which contains three parallel modules for the first ten weeks followed by one integrating module for the final five weeks, in which students are put into groups and given a task specifically designed to integrate the learning from the preceding three parallel modules. In the Australian university's terms, this final integrating module would be an excellent example of a cornerstone module.

3. The first year of a UK automotive engineering course has one substantial year-long module to build a working go-cart. In each of the three terms, there are also smaller term-long modules covering different subjects vital to that central purpose and therefore contributing directly to that core module. I'm not sure whether, in the Australian university's terms that central module would be deemed a cornerstone or a capstone but it would certainly be one or other.

Reconsider how best to record summative assessment of learning outcomes

In my view, one of the greatest scandals in university education around the world is the perpetuation of indefensible unscholarly marking practices and assessment systems, primarily based on the statistically illiterate misuse of numbers (Rust, 2007; 2011; & previous chapter). The logic of an outcomes-based approach to course design requires that the assessment should test whether the outcomes have been achieved and therefore the sole criterion necessary should be "has the outcome been met?" Yet most assessment systems around the world persist in grading or, even worse, percentage marking suggesting a level of precision that is not humanly possible. They also often tend to use criteria that bear little direct relation to the espoused outcomes. Then they aggregate these results. This is done despite the fact that they assessed different things, and the ranges will have been different, thus obscuring the different types of learning outcome purportedly represented by the separate scores.

There is considerable research evidence showing how unreliable marking can be (e.g. Laming,1990; Newstead & Dennis,1994; Newstead, 2002), and not just between markers, but even as individuals, the same marker often giving a different mark to the same piece of work if marked again after a gap of time (Hartog & Rhodes,1935; Hanlon et al, 2004). Essentially, *"Grades are inherently ambiguous evaluations of performance with no absolute connection to educational achievement"* (Felton & Koper, 2005 p562).

But stubbornly, the higher education sector continues to ignore this research on the unreliability of marking, and the unscholarly marking and grading practices, even though this is at a great cost, particularly in terms of staff time. The result is vast quantities of unreliable and unhelpful data, which nevertheless is treated as objective truth and affects students' lives and careers.

In terms of the primary purpose of summative assessment – making decisions about progression, qualification, license to practice, etc. – we don't need anywhere near the amount of data most programmes produce, and arguably this surfeit unhelpfully creates a 'wood-for-the-trees' situation. Far fewer, but more rigorous, assessment results would enable better decisions and save considerable amounts of staff time. Trying to decide if a piece of work deserves 63 or 64 is not time well spent!

My recommendation to any programme team is to seriously consider whether summative assessment decisions need to be anything more than pass/fail, or possibly pass/merit/distinction if some kind of ranking is deemed to be desirable. And if this is seen as just too radical a step to take, at least consider the following compromise. If you have accepted the earlier arguments for 'programme-focussed assessment', 'curriculum sequencing' and for the need for 'building-block' modules, why not at least restrict summative grading to the cornerstone and capstone modules, where the focus is on programme outcomes, and the assessment of integrated learning is taking place (in the UK they could be classed as 'honours' modules) and make all the other modules essentially formative by simply assessing them pass/fail?

WHAT WE THINK WE KNOW....

Make summative assessment tasks more effective

Once the programme team has dealt with the big picture, ensuring constructive alignment and curriculum sequencing across the programme, attention should then be given to the quality of the summative assessment tasks to be used. There are arguably three linked, but different, qualities that can help to make the task effective:

- Validity – does the task truly assess what you claim it assesses? Writing a 500 word essay on "How to give safe injections" would not actually assess whether a nursing student could give safe injections
- Authenticity‡ – is it 'real' world task? Does it look like something someone might ever be expected to do in a setting outside the university? And such tasks can be even more effective if they can actually be undertaken in a 'real' world setting such as a placements, or by undertaking a 'live' project (so literally doing it 'for real')
- Relevance – can the student see why this topic is important? Why they need to know this? How it fits with the rest of the subject and the bigger picture? And even better if there can be personal relevance and it can be something which the student is personally interested in, and wants to know more about or be able to do – so can there be elements of choice about the task/s undertaken?

Both authenticity and relevance should make the activity meaningful to the student, and there is strong of research evidence that that should therefore increase the likelihood that the student will be motivated to engage with the task (the exact antithesis of what common parlance means by an 'academic exercise', namely something that is essentially pointless!)

‡Marilyn Lombardi (2007) provides a very useful checklist, distilling the 10 design elements of the authentic learning experience:

1. *Real-world relevance*: Authentic activities match the real-world tasks of professionals in practice as nearly as possible. Learning rises to the level of authenticity when it asks students to work actively with abstract concepts, facts, and formulae inside a realistic— and highly social—context mimicking "the ordinary practices of the [disciplinary] culture."[7]

2. *Ill-defined problem*: Challenges cannot be solved easily by the application of an existing algorithm; instead, authentic activities are relatively undefined and open to multiple interpretations, requiring students to identify for themselves the tasks and subtasks needed to complete the major task.
3. *Sustained investigation*: Problems cannot be solved in a matter of minutes or even hours. Instead, authentic activities comprise complex tasks to be investigated by students over a sustained period of time, requiring significant investment of time and intellectual resources.
4. *Multiple sources and perspectives*: Learners are not given a list of resources. Authentic activities provide the opportunity for students to examine the task from a variety of theoretical and practical perspectives, using a variety of resources, and requires students to distinguish relevant from irrelevant information in the process.
5. *Collaboration*: Success is not achievable by an individual learner working alone. Authentic activities make collaboration integral to the task, both within the course and in the real world.
6. *Reflection (metacognition)*: Authentic activities enable learners to make choices and reflect on their learning, both individually and as a team or community.
7. *Interdisciplinary perspective*: Relevance is not confined to a single domain or subject matter specialization. Instead, authentic activities have consequences that extend beyond a particular discipline, encouraging students to adopt diverse roles and think in interdisciplinary terms.
8. *Integrated assessment*: Assessment is not merely summative in authentic activities but is woven seamlessly into the major task in a manner that reflects real-world evaluation processes.
9. 9. *Polished products*: Conclusions are not merely exercises or substeps in preparation for something else. Authentic activities culminate in the creation of a whole product, valuable in its own right.
10. 10. *Multiple interpretations and outcomes*: Rather than yielding a single correct answer obtained by the application of rules and procedures, authentic activities allow for diverse interpretations and competing solutions.

WHAT WE THINK WE KNOW....

Creating a community of assessment practice

For faculty

In order to achieve any degree of marker reliability, it is necessary to bring the markers into a community of assessment practice. In the UK, this was recognised by the Higher Education Quality Council (the precursor to the Quality Assurance Agency) twenty years ago:

> *"Consistent assessment decisions among assessors are the product of interactions over time, the internalisation of exemplars, and of inclusive networks. Written instructions, mark schemes and criteria, even when used with scrupulous care, cannot substitute for these"* (HEQC, 1997)

It is, therefore, slightly surprising to observe that much of the emphasis of the QAA and quality assurance since then has in fact been on the latter activities, with ever greater requirements for instructions, marking schemes and criteria to be in writing. Recently, however, especially in exploratory work in Australia, there seems to have been a growing recognition for the need for these social processes highlighted by HEQC and for markers' judgements to be 'calibrated' (Sadler, 2012; Watty et al, 2013). If programme teams are to ensure the best possible reliability of their assessment decisions, it can only be achieved by the programme instituting internal, faculty calibration processes.

For students

But it is also vital that the students are brought into this community of assessment practice, specifically, as a key aspect of the wider disciplinary community of practice, for a number of linked, but distinct reasons.

Firstly, there is the fairly basic argument of Sadler that an indispensable condition for improvement in student learning is that *"the student comes to hold a concept of quality roughly similar to that held by the teacher"* (Sadler, 1989). The sooner the students understands what counts as 'good' work the better, as they will then be able to produce better work. And this acculturation regarding standards is best developed through participation because *"participation, as a way of learning, enables the student to both absorb, and be absorbed in the culture of practice*" (Elwood & Klenowski, 2002, p. 246).

Secondly, this is arguably the key to solving the feedback dilemma currently plaguing higher education. That dilemma being that all the research evidence suggests that potentially feedback has a crucial role to play in the assessment cycle in supporting and developing students' learning, but in reality students are hugely critical of our feedback practices, and the quality of the feedback they receive, and therefore tend not to engage with it (Price et al, 2010; O'Donovan et al, 2015). There have been a growing number of studies that show that the passive receipt of feedback has little effect on future performance (e.g. Fritz et al, 2000) and that dialogue and participatory relationships are key elements of engaging students with assessment feedback (e.g. ESwAF FDTL, 2007). But sadly many attempts by institutions to address the feedback dilemma have ignored this research choosing instead to try and improve the existing practices. This could be characterised by the mantra 'more feedback quicker!' But this completely ignores David Boud's apposite observation that feedback that has no 'effect' cannot be seen as feedback – it is simply input (Boud and Molloy, 2012)). Given the evidence that much, current feedback is not engaged with by the students, is largely ignored and has no discernible effect on the students' subsequent work (e.g. Hounsell, 1987; Fritz, 2000; MacLellan, 2001) – more of what we are doing, however quick, is not going to improve feedback.

Why the 'more, quicker' approach is ineffective and almost certainly doomed to only very limited success, if not failure, is also eloquently addressed by David Nicol when he says that it is not sufficient to make feedback a better 'monologue' – feedback must be seen as a dialogue (Nicol, 2010). And he goes on to say that it is not pedantry to point out that, technically, a dialogue is not just two people (that's a duologue) - it is three or more. He is not arguing simply to turn feedback into a conversation between student and tutor – it needs to go much wider than that, including student with student, in the wider community of practice.

Finally, there is powerful research evidence that there is a direct correlation between student involvement and engagement in interactions at all levels with others in the programme (both faculty and students), and their academic success. Based on the huge database provided by the US National Survey of Student Engagement, Astin has shown that the most significant factor in student academic success is student involvement, fostered by student/staff interactions and student/student interactions (both formal and informal) (Astin, 1997). And a study by Graham Gibbs, trying to identify what departments in elite universities around the world, rated highly for both their teaching and their research, had in common, concluded that the only identifiable similarity was high levels of student involvement (Gibbs et al, 2008).

I would argue that a major benefit to the student, gained through interaction and involvement, which helps to explain their subsequent academic success, is the acquisition of 'assessment literacy'. If the students are to reach their true potential in terms of their assessed performance the cultivated development of the students' assessment literacy should therefore be of prime importance to the programme team in planning a programme's assessment.

Assessment literacy encompasses:

- an appreciation of assessment's relationship to learning;
- a conceptual understanding of assessment (i.e. understanding of the basic principles of valid assessment and feedback practice, including the terminology used);
- understanding of the nature, meaning and level of assessment criteria and standards;
- skills in self and peer assessment;
- familiarity with technical approaches to assessment (i.e. familiarity with pertinent assessment and feedback skills, techniques, and methods, including their purpose and efficacy); and
- possession of the intellectual ability to select and apply appropriate approaches and techniques to assessed tasks (not only does one have the requisite skills, but one is also able to judge which skill to use when, for which task).

(Price et al, 2012 pp10-11)

It should be noted that students undertaking multidisciplinary degrees may well be compelled to negotiate between the different assessment literacies bound up in the different disciplinary cultures and practices, and this needs to be explicitly recognised by the faculty involved.

Central to the development of assessment literacy is the involvement of students in self and peer assessment, and the opportunities this offers for all-important dialogue about assessment. Involving students in the assessment process is not a new idea, and has been widely introduced and researched (e.g. Falchikov, 2004). What is needed is a conceptual shift whereby a commitment is made, at the programme-level, to the planned development of student assessment literacy (or literacies in a multidisciplinary programme). This will, in turn, require the programme team to make strategic decisions at the programme and planning and design stage, about the use of self- and peer-assessment. Such an approach pre-empts an approach that relies on the interest, enthusiasm or skill of individual module leader who may, if permitted to make module design decisions in isolation from considerations of the student experience and programme design, choose to use or reject self- and peer-assessment as potential ways of varying the design of assessment tasks.

There is also a strong connection between assessment literacy and the employability agenda [and what David Boud, in Australia, has termed "sustainable assessment" – see https://www.uts.edu.au/sites/default/files/davidboudKeynote.pdf accessed 1/9/20]. A key aspect of employability is critical self-awareness – the *"students' awareness of the [graduate] attributes and their understanding of their own personal development of the attributes"* (Rust and Froud, 2016 p9). Put simply, it is surely an essential attribute of a graduate and/or a professional to be able to assess the quality of their own work and also the quality of the work of their colleagues and peers?

And there is a further clear connection between graduate employability and authentic learning and assessment. Lombardi (2007, p9) argues it can play a crucial role in helping to develop the largely overlooked 'conate domain' (the capacity to act, decide and commit) *"which determines whether a student has the necessary will, desire, commitment, mental energy, and self-determination to actually perform at the highest disciplinary standards. By engaging students in issues of concern to them, from global warming to world hunger, authentic learning awakens in learners the confidence to act."* She further cites (p10) that, *"according to Frank Levy and Richard Murnane (2005), expert thinking and complex communication* [developed by authentic learning] *will differentiate those with career-transcending skills from those who have little opportunity for advancement."*

More formative assessment and improving the effectiveness of feedback

If we are to maximise the potential of feedback to support and improve student learning, there needs to be an increase in formative assessment opportunities, where students can learn from their mistakes, and possibly take risks without jeopardising their final grades. While, as previously stated, it is unquestionably true that 'we assess too much' when it comes to summative assessment, given that formative assessment is primarily focussed on learning, there can't really be too much formative assessment – that would be like saying 'we have too much learning'. This, of course, comes with the caveat – providing that the overall work-demand on the students (i.e. expected total student learning hours) is realistic. And if the potential benefit of formative assessment tasks is to be maximised, the students will need effective feedback, whether that comes from the tutor, themselves and/or their peers.

Val Shute, in the US, memorably argues that if feedback is to be effective, you need 'MOM' – Motive, Opportunity, and Means (Shute, 2008). To engage with feedback students need to be motivated, and that is much more likely if they will have an opportunity, in the foreseeable future, to put the feedback into practice. This can be in the form of having another go, either redoing the same piece of work or undertaking a new but similar task. Even if this is achieved, however, she argues that it may well not be effective in helping to improve the student's work. If, for example, your feedback tells them that their analysis is not very good, this may help to explain any indicative grade given but it doesn't help the student analyse better. Their analysis may well not be very good because they don't understand exactly what you mean by analysis, or what good analysis looks like. In order to undertake better analysis they need the 'means' to help them. And depending on context, this could take all manner of forms – 'come and see me for a tutorial', 'suggest you re-read chapter three of the text book', 'go and look at x on the course website', etc.

David Nicol (University of Strathclyde) advises that when you start designing a course, as well as considering the constructive alignment of the summative assessment, early consideration should be given to designing what preceding, formative assessment will be undertaken, and that explicit feedback loops should be built in. [For detailed, practical examples of ways to increase formative assessment and to improve the effectiveness of feedback look at the REAP project at Strathclyde – www.reap.ac.uk accessed 1/9/20 - and also O'Donovan et al, 2015]

Given that if tutor feedback is to be done well it can be expensive, particularly in terms of time, a review of resource allocation, with a view to focussing resources on high-value feedback where it can have the most impact on student learning, is recommended The points at which such feedback is of most value is likely to be where the students are most challenged – points of 'troublesome knowledge', where they may be confronted by epistemological jumps and/or where there are changes in the levels of support and autonomy (O'Donovan, 2010).

Summary

This chapter argues that student achievement could be improved, and many of the persistent problems with assessment in universities overcome, if a strategic approach is taken to the design of the course programme and its assessment.

In particular, this approach should:

- develop a common philosophy
- ensure both that the programme is constructively aligned, and the curriculum 'sequenced' with 'building block' modules, identifying explicitly where the programme's outcomes and integrated learning are assessed
- ensure that staff and students understand the programme's philosophy, and the raison d'être of the programme structure
- reduce the summative assessment points, focussing them explicitly on the assessment of the programme outcomes, and improve the rigour and quality of those assessments

- adopt as simple a grade-based marking system as your institution will allow
- increase the opportunities for formative assessment, and actively engage students in the assessment process, especially through dialogue, with the specific intention of developing their assessment literacy and improving the effectiveness of assessment feedback.
- Explicitly recognise the ability to self and peer assess as an essential graduate outcome

Arguably, none of this should actually be difficult. And ridiculously, probably the hardest requirement for many programmes will be the initial bringing together of faculty concerned, getting them to see themselves as a programme team, and to accept the idea of jointly, collaboratively, designing the programme together. And if anything this is arguable getting harder as staff become more isolated in narrowly focused departmental structures built around research rather than teaching demands (Macfarlane, 2011).

Bibliography

Astin, A. (1997) *What matters in college? Four critical years revisited*. San Francisco: Jossey Bass.

Biggs, J. (1999) *Teaching for quality learning at university*, Buckingham: SRHE & Open University Press

Boud, D. (1995) Assessment and learning: Contradictory or complementary? In P. Knight (Ed*) Assessment for Learning in Higher Education*, 35-48, London: Kogan Page)

Boud, D. & Molly, M. (2012) Rethinking models of feedback for learning: the challenge of design, *Assessment & Evaluation in Higher Education*, 38 (6)

Burgess A, Senior C, Moores E (2018) A 10-year case study on the changing determinants of university student satisfaction in the UK. *PLoS ONE* 13 (2): e0192976. Accessed 1/9/20 at:
https://journals.plos.org/plosone/article?id=10.1371/journal.pone.0192976

Dressel, P.L. (1957) Facts and fancy in assigning grades, *Basic College Quarterly*, Winter 6-12

Elwood, J. and Klenowski, V. (2002) Creating communities of shared practice: the challenges of assessment use in learning and teaching, *Assessment and Evaluation in*

Higher Education, 27, 243-256.

ESwAF FDTL (2007), 'Final Report'. Available online at: https://mw.brookes.ac.uk/display/eswaf/Home

Falchikov, N. (2004) *Improving Assessment Through Student Involvement: Practical Solutions for Higher and Further Education Teaching and Learning*, London: Routledge Falmer

Felton, J. & Koper, P.T. (2005) Nominal GPA and real GPA: a simple adjustment that compensates for grade inflation, *Assessment and Evaluation in Higher Education*, 30 (6), 561-69

Fritz, C.O., Morris, P.E., Bjork, R.A., Gelman, R. and Wickens, T.D. (2000) When further learning fails: stability and change following repeated presentation of text, *British Journal of Psychology*, 91, 493-511.

Gibbs, G. et al (2008) Disciplinary and contextually appropriate approaches to leadership of teaching in research-intensive academic departments in higher education, *Higher Education Quarterly,* 62 (4), 416–436.

Hanlon, J., Jefferson, M., Molan, M. and Mitchell, B (2004) *An examination of the incidence of 'error variation' in the grading of law assessments,* United Kingdom Centre for Legal Education

Hartog, P. & Rhodes, E. C. (1935) *An Examination of Examinations,* London: Macmillan

Havnes, A (2008). *There is a bigger story behind. An analysis of mark average variation across programmes.* European Association for Research into Learning and Instruction Assessment Conference, University of Northumbria.

Higher Education Quality Council (1997) *Assessment in higher education and the role of 'graduateness',* London: HEQC.

Hounsell, D. (1987) Essay Writing and the Quality of Feedback. In *Student Learning: Research in Education and Cognitive Psychology*, edited by J. T. E. Richardson, M. W. Eysenck, and D. Warren-Piper, 101–108. Milton Keynes: Open University Press.

Laming, D. (1990) 'The reliability of a certain university examination compared with the precision of absolute judgments', *Quarterly Journal of Experimental Psychology*, vol. 42 pp. 239-254

Langan MA, Dunleavy P, Fielding A. (2013) Applying Models to National Surveys of Undergraduate Science Students: What Affects Ratings of Satisfaction? *Educ Sci.* 3(2).

Levy, F. & Murnane, R (2005) *The new division of labor: How computers are creating the next job market*, Princeton, NJ: Princeton University Press

Lombardi, Marilyn M. (2007) *Authentic Learning for the 21st Century: an overview*, ELI paper 1, Educause Learning Initiative,
Accessed 1/9/20 at
https://www.researchgate.net/publication/220040581_Authentic_Learning_for_the_21st_Century_An_Overview

Macfarlane, B. (2011). The Morphing of Academic Practice: Unbundling and the Rise of the Para-academic, *Higher Education Quarterly,* 65 (1), 59–73.

MacLellan, E. (2001). Assessment for Learning: The Differing Perceptions of Tutors and Students, *Assessment and Evaluation in Higher Education* 26 (4), 307–318.

Mascolo, M.F. & Castillo, J. (2015). The origins of underperformance in Higher Education in America: proximal systems of influence. *Pedagogy and the Human Sciences*, 5 (1), 1-40

Newstead, S.E. & Dennis, I. (1994) Examiners examined: the reliability of exam marking in psychology. *The Psychologist*, 7, 216-219.

Newstead, S. (2002) Examining the examiners: why are we so bad at assessing students? *Psychology Learning and Teaching*, 2 (2), 70-75

Nicol, D (2010) From monologue to dialogue: improving written feedback in mass higher education, *Assessment and Evaluation in Higher Education*, 35 (5), pp 501-517.

O'Donovan, B. (2010) Filling the Pail or Lighting a Fire? The Intellectual Development of Management Students, *International Journal of Management Education* 9 (1): 1–10.

O'Donovan, B., Rust, C. & Price, P. (2015) A scholarly approach to solving the feedback dilemma in practice, *Assessment & Evaluation in Higher Education* Accessed 1/9/20 at
https://www.researchgate.net/publication/278390380_A_scholarly_approach_to_solving_the_feedback_dilemma_in_practice

O'Neill, G., Donnelly, R., & Fitzmaurice, M. (2014) Supporting Programme Teams to Develop Sequencing in Higher Education Curricula, *International Journal of Academic Development,* 19 (4) Accessed 1/9/20 at
http://www.tandfonline.com/doi/full/10.1080/1360144X.2013.867266

Price, M., Handley, K., Millar, J., & O'Donovan, B. (2010) Feedback: all that effort, but what is the effect?. *Assessment & Evaluation in Higher Education*, 35 (3), 277-289.

Price, M., Rust, C., O'Donovan, B., Handley, K. with Bryant, R. (2012) *Assessment literacy: the foundation for improving student learning*, Oxford: Oxford Centre for Staff and Learning Development

Rust, C. (2007) 'Towards a scholarship of assessment', *Assessment and Evaluation in Higher Education,* Vol. 32 (2), 229-237

Rust, C. (2011) The unscholarly use of numbers in our assessment practices; what will make us change? *International Journal for the Scholarship of Teaching and Learning,* 5 (1), January 2011.
Accessed 1/9/20 at: https://digitalcommons.georgiasouthern.edu/ij-sotl/vol5/iss1/4/

Rust, C., & Froud, L. (2016) "Shifting the focus from skills to 'graduateness'" *Phoenix,* Issue 148, June, 8-9 Accessed 1/9/20 at:
https://www.researchgate.net/publication/303975538_Shifting_the_focus_from_skills_to_%27graduateness%27

Sadler, D. R. (1989) Formative assessment and the design of instructional systems, *Instructional Science*, 18, 119-144.

Sadler, D.R. (2013) Assuring academic achievement standards: From moderation to calibration. *Assessment in Education: Principles, Policy and Practice*, 20 (1), 5-19

Shute, V. 2008. Focus on Formative Feedback, *Review of Educational Research* 78 (1), 153–189.

Watty, K., Freeman, M., Howieson, B., Hancock, P., O'Connell, B., de Lange, P., and Abraham, A. (2014) Social moderation, assessment and assuring standards for accounting graduates, *Assessment & Evaluation in Higher Education* 39 (4).
DOI: 10.1080/02602938.2013.848336

5 Avoiding the road to hell: the need to evaluate our practice and to corroborate what we think we know.

For me, the overarching message of this chapter is not to take things we think we know for granted, and certainly not to trust in practices just because they're common or traditional, or to be unquestioningly seduced by arguments based on apparent 'common sense'. It is vital that we evaluate our own practice and that strategic decisions, and proposed changes in practice, are evidence-based. In addition to that, once a piece of research is completed, we should never assume that the matter is over and resolved but rather we should continue to monitor and constantly keep our practice under review. This is especially important if we are to avoid the danger of unintended consequences.

As someone now retired, who spent almost thirty years in educational development, I have been looking back reflectively on changes in the sector, many of which I have been a part of, and I find a somewhat depressing theme emerges – which I am summarising as *the road to hell.* According to the proverb, the road to hell is paved with good intentions, and it seems to me that there is a growing amount of pedagogic research evidence showing that many of the pedagogic problems and issues that we are facing now can actually be traced back to very well intentioned and logically advocated innovations which have suffered from the law of unintended consequences. And often, I'd suggest, the logic of those changes was based on thinking that there are easy answers to what in fact are highly complex problems.

Don't get me wrong; I am not advocating inertia as preferable to action in the absence of evidence. Sometimes inaction may be the worst possible choice and maybe we have to take an 'educated' step in to the dark. But even more important in such situations is that we monitor and evaluate (research) the effects of any changes that we make.

Continuous assessment is one of the innovations I have in mind. Compared with a system of final exams, which is very high-stakes and consequently stressful, and may also encourage students to leave serious study until too late, how much better to have regular assessment, structuring learning and giving students regular feedback on how well they are doing? These are powerful and well-meaning arguments.

In a similar vein, came the case for **modularity** – the chunking-up of knowledge packages into bite-size units of learning. Rather than one, centrally imposed linear curriculum with little if any choice either as to what is studied, or how or when, modularity could give the students both flexibility and choice. In addition, there may be economies of scale with students from a variety of programmes taking the same module, making it viable. And with the introduction of the concept of CATS (Credit Accumulation and Transfer), there could be the additional flexibility of being able to dip in and out of learning, as has long happened in the US, and providing greater mobility too through the ease of transference from one institution to another. What could possibly be wrong with that?

But what has been the reality of these changes? The combination of continuous assessment and credit accumulation through modular/unitised systems has arguably contributed significantly to students becoming largely, if not totally, focussed on the marks received for any given piece of work, rather than the feedback on the learning achieved that they are meant to represent (Newstead, 2002). Instrumentalist students in modular systems are likely to adopt a "tick box" mentality, moving on to the next unit or module without seeing any connection between past and future learning (Rust, 2000).

Continuous assessment also encourages students to "play safe" in the work that they do. If it is going to count, do you really want to risk losing marks by doing something a bit different or in an area you are less good at? From a course programme point of view, it arguably has made it much harder to ensure continuity and development within the curriculum, or to allow for "slow learning" (Claxton, 1998), as well as making it harder to assess complex outcomes or to assess integrated learning (McDowell, 2012).

Modularity/unitisation has certainly increased summative assessment to the point that it is now a cliché in the sector to say that students are over-assessed while, because of reductions in resourcing, and the shortness of modules, and pressures on staff time there is arguably less formative assessment, with feedback focusing on justifying the mark given (Price et al, 2008). None of these outcomes would have been wanted by the original advocates for the changes and, ironically, very few modular systems in the UK ever really succeeded in providing meaningful course choices. And the transferability and flexibility potentially offered by CATS has hardly been utilised – although we may now, at least according to some enthusiasts, finally be entering an era of MOOCs and 'edupunks' when it just might be.

It is also important to acknowledge that both ideas aren't without some merit, and it's unlikely they would have been advocated if they were. Continuous *formative* assessment providing regular feedback is evidently good practice – it is excessive continuous *summative* assessment that causes these problems with learning. Modularity too undoubtedly has positive aspects. Its problems stem from a lack of programme level design. Both innovations had positive elements but were introduced piecemeal, without sufficient consideration of their wider effects and the 'bigger picture'.

Learning outcomes, assessment criteria and greater clarity and transparency generally are another set of innovations we have seen in the last 30 years - and again, in response to some very good arguments. Staff will deliver better courses if they are clear about what they are doing and students have a right to know what the course is about and trying to achieve and the outcomes expected of them. It will also be easier for it to be assessed and for assessment feedback to be focused around the outcomes and with reference to the criteria. And it will all be easier to hold to account for quality assurance. So what on earth is wrong with all that?! Well, when it comes to assessment I know with embarrassment (given the work I did in the 90s trying to develop and promote these very ideas) that this desire for explicitness has led to the creation of assessment grids that try to define each possible grade for each criterion sometimes, at worst, with set numbers of marks allocated for each criterion. While such grids may be useful as a checklist for a marker, and also in the focusing of feedback to a student, their more rigid application may ignore the holistic nature of assessment (Sadler, 2005), and the tacit components within the assessment decision. The use of such grids will not, on their own, improve students' understanding of what is required of them or improve the quality of their work, can distract from focusing on the learning outcomes, and when coupled with marks may totally distort the assessment outcome and bear little if any relationship to the learning outcomes supposedly being assessed (Price & Rust, 1999; O'Donovan et al, 2000; Rust, 2011).

There is also evidence that students knowing too much about what is expected of them in terms of assessment may lead to them doing only that, safe in the knowledge of what they need to do to meet the minimum requirements required to pass the module, thereby reducing the amount of student effort and subsequent learning (Gibbs & Dunbar-Godet, 2007)

Again, arguably none of these issues are inherently the fault of the original 'good idea'. The positive arguments for learning outcomes identified above certainly do exist. The problem is the way they have been (mis)used, their over zealous use in QA procedures and in trying to control processes and behaviours – and also, again, in terms of course planning and design.

A further associated change in assessment practices has been an increase in the *variety of assessment methods used*. This happened for a number of reasons – the recognition that traditional assessment methods such as exams and essays can't assess everything we should be assessing and a desire for greater validity and authenticity. There was also an argument that every assessment practice disadvantaged somebody so variety would at least even out that disadvantage. So what's wrong with variety? Well there's probably nothing necessarily wrong with variety itself but there can be, and especially too much variety. If students are to make use of the feedback they receive, and to learn from their mistakes, they need an opportunity, relatively soon, to put that feedback into practice and to have another go at a similar piece of work, and maybe more than once, to refine their understanding and skills.

In **summation**, I think the common thread in what I'm saying is that many innovations of the last thirty years or so have been made, in the absence of hard evidence, on the basis of well-reasoned arguments attempting to address identifiable problems. They have had negative, unintended consequences, not because the reasoning was necessarily flawed but often because they have tried to offer simple solutions to complex problems, and then not been sufficiently monitored and judiciously 'tinkered with' after their introduction. Neither has their effect on the 'bigger picture' been effectively monitored and evaluated from the beginning, and they may well have also been confounded by higher-level factors, and in some cases they have been used in other initially unforeseen ways.

Another more recent example of what I am trying to say is the move, vigorously supported by the NUS, to anonymous marking. Again, there are apparently good reasons. Some studies have undoubtedly shown that markers who know the identity of the student are capable of bias, and that this may especially have negative consequences for certain groups of students. Clearly this is an issue that needs to be addressed. But the campaign for anonymous marking ignores the research data that emphasises the importance of a relationship between marker and student if feedback is to be seriously engaged with and attended to (Handley et al, 2008; Nicol, 2010). So instead of a knee-jerk move to universal anonymity, more subtle and nuanced solutions need to be developed. One excellent example of that is anonymous marking with personalised feedback: i.e. the work is originally marked anonymously and, once decided upon, an unchangeable mark/grade is entered into the system which then, and only then, reveals the student's identity so that the marker can then write personalised feedback.

And I guess this last example illustrates what I see as the conclusion to these reflections. If we are to avoid unintended consequences and to continue paving the road to hell, we must acknowledge that it is not sufficient just to have good reasons to want to change something – we must insist on pedagogic research evidence that supports the change regarding the potential consequences. And if none exists we need pilot studies and to publish and disseminate the results of those studies, including our failures as well as our successes. We also need to make sure that we are tackling the right problem.

Bibliography

Claxton, G. (1998) *Hare brain, tortoise mind*, London; Fourth Estate

Gibbs, G. and Dunbar-Goddet, H. (2007) *The effects of programme assessment environments on student learning*, Oxford Learning Institute, Oxford: University of Oxford. Accessed 1/9/20 at: https://www.advance-he.ac.uk/knowledge-hub/effects-programme-assessment-environments-student-learning

Handley, K., Price, M. and Millar, J. (2008) *Engaging Students with Assessment Feedback: Final Report for FDTL5 Project 144/03,* Oxford; Oxford Brookes University

McDowell, Liz. (2012) *Programme Focused Assessment: a short guide*, Bradford; PASS Project Accessed 1/9/20 at : https://www.bradford.ac.uk/pass/resources/short-guide.pdf

Newstead, S. (2002) Examining the examiners: why are we so bad at assessing students? *Psychology Learning and Teaching*, 2 (2) pp. 70-75

Nicol, D. (2010) From monologue to dialogue: improving written feedback processes in mass higher education, *Assessment & Evaluation in Higher Education* 35 (5) pp. 501-

517

O'Donovan, B., Price, M. & Rust, C. (2000) The student experience of criterion-referenced assessment (through the introduction of a common criteria assessment grid), *Innovation in Education and Teaching International*, 38 (1) pp. 74-85.

Price, M., O'Donovan, B., Rust, C. & Carroll, J. (2008) Assessment Standards: A Manifesto for Change, *Brookes eJournal of Learning and Teaching.* 2 (3) Accessed 1/9/20 at: https://www.advance-he.ac.uk/knowledge-hub/assessment-standards-manifesto-change

Price, M. and Rust, C. (1999) The experience of introducing a common criteria assessment grid across an academic department, *Quality in Higher Education*, 5 (2) pp. 133-144.

Rust, C. (2000) An opinion piece: A possible student-centred assessment solution to some of the current problems of modular degree programmes, *Active Learning in Higher Education,* 1 (2) pp. 126-131

Rust, C. (2011) The Unscholarly Use of Numbers in Our Assessment Practices: What Will Make Us Change? *International Journal for the Scholarship of Teaching and Learning*, 5 (1) Accessed 1/9/20 at:
https://digitalcommons.georgiasouthern.edu/cgi/viewcontent.cgi?article=1254&context=ij-sotl

Sadler, D. R. (2005) Interpretations of criteria-based assessment and grading in higher education, *Assessment and Evaluation in Higher Education*, 30 pp. 175 - 194

ABOUT THE AUTHOR

Chris Rust is Emeritus Professor of Higher Education at Oxford Brookes where he worked for over 25 years. He was Head of the Oxford Centre for Staff and Learning Development, and Deputy Director of the Human Resource Directorate from 2001-2011. Between 2005-10 he was also Deputy Director for two Centres for Excellence in Teaching and Learning - ASKe (Assessment Standards Knowledge Exchange) and the Reinvention Centre for undergraduate research (led by Warwick University). For his last three years there he was Associate Dean (Academic Policy)

He has researched and published on a range of issues including:

- the experiences of new teachers in HE
- the positive effects of supplemental instruction
- the effectiveness of workshops as a method of staff development.
- ways of diversifying assessment
- improving student performance through engagement in the assessment process

He has been a Fellow of the RSA, a Senior Fellow of SEDA (Staff and Educational Development Association) and was one of the first fourteen Senior Fellows of the UK Higher Education Academy.

In 2015, he was a member of a team that reviewed external examining arrangements in the UK and since 2016 he has been a member of the Advance HE *Degree standards* project team.

He has also published an extended short story for teenagers called *Piglet*

Printed in Great Britain
by Amazon